A SWORD BATHED IN HEAVEN

A SWORD BATHED IN

HEAVEN

The Life, faith and cruel death of the
Rev. Robert Bradford B.Th. M.P.

NORAH BRADFORD

Pickering Paperbacks

Marshall Pickering
3 Beggarwood Lane, Basingstoke, Hants, RG23 7LP, UK

First published by Pickering and Inglis 1984

Reprinted
Impression number
84 85 86 87 : 6 5 4 3 2

British Library Cataloguing in Publication Data
Bradford, Norah
   A sword bathed in heaven: the life, faith and cruel
   death of Robert Bradford, MP.
   1. Bradford, Robert 2. Politicians—
   Northern Ireland—Biography
   941.6082'092'4   DA990.U452B7

ISBN 0 7208 0580 5

Typeset by Spire Print Services Ltd, Salisbury, Wilts

Printed and bound in Great Britain by
Anchor Brendon Limited, Tiptree, Essex

Cover photograph by Pacemaker Press
Photograph of author by Trevor Harvey

To the glory of God.

To Sadie Nicholson

and

To the memory of 'Wee Jimmy' Nicholson,
Aunt Liz and Uncle Bob.

ACKNOWLEDGEMENTS

My grateful thanks to my friend, prayer partner, chief critic and typist Noëlle Millar, without whose patient work and gentle criticism this book might never have been written.

My thanks to Derick and Margaret Bingham for their helpful suggestions and persevering reading and re-reading of the manuscript, and for their immeasurable encouragement from the beginning.

My thanks also to Ben and Lily Ford for their helpfulness in so many ways.

My thanks to the many friends who have faithfully prayed for me throughout the writing of this book.

To protect certain individuals who feature in this book, their real identities are concealed and fictitious names are used.

INTRODUCTION

Robert felt his task on this earth was a particularly difficult one, especially in the political field.

This is how Robert saw the part he had to play,

'My role is to say harsh things oft times, but to bathe the sharp sword of my words in heaven, to temper what I say with love, and lead people from their folly to a life of fuller service with the King.'

Robert had been elected to the Westminster Parliament for the second time and we were now feeling slightly more secure.

I was in the kitchen peeling potatoes when Robert found me that day.

'What does that passage of scripture say to you?' he said holding out his bible. I dried my hands and took the book.

'Which passage?' I said.

'Read from there,' he pointed.

I sat down on the high breakfast bar stool and read.

I looked up and saw by his white strained face that it meant the same to him.

I read it again.

'It says you're going to be shot.' I spoke in a whisper. I carried on quickly as much to convince myself as him. 'Many people got shot and they're OK again, look at John Taylor. It doesn't say killed, maybe it just means wounded.'

It was some years later on a crisp clear November day that I stood at the front door watching our two small dogs romp around the green grass. I had no way of knowing that it was to be this day that my husband was to enter Glory. That he was to be suddenly snatched from this realm into Higher

Service, there to stand at the feet of his Saviour.
   This is the story of his life and faith.

Norah Bradford
Upper Malone
Belfast
June 1984

1

Even in the sunshine his three-piece suit looked dowdy and old-fashioned. 'That's Robert Bradford' someone said. His fair curly hair cropped very short doesn't suit him, I thought. 'Should I know him?' I said out loud. 'You know, the Edgehill student,' she urged.

That Summer School week of 1964 at Mourne Grange, Kilkeel made a tremendous impression on me. At sixteen I was suddenly a person in my own right. Not being introduced as someone's daughter or sister was important. People wanted to know me as just me. I made many friends and enjoyed the fellowship of other young people seeking the Lord. At communion service on that last Sunday in the little grey chapel in the grounds an appeal was made for anyone wanting to commit their life to the Lord, and I knew that that meant me. I couldn't wait to get up to that communion rail. I know I stood on toes trying to get out of those narrow wooden pews, but I hadn't time to wait for people to move. I trembled in the presence of the Lord as I knelt at this feet and committed my life into his hands.

It was over a year later that I met Robert face to face. The Belfast group's Summer School reunion in October was held in our school chaplain's house. We had a time of Bible study and prayer and then supper and a chance to chat. I was talking to my friend Barbara, seated cross-legged on the floor, when I became aware of him watching me. I blushed and continued talking, trying to ignore those smiling light brown eyes framed in thick dark rimmed spectacles. Barbara turned to him and he joined in the conversation. I in turn watched him. There was sparkle and life in this boy that I had missed seeing that summer's day the year before.

The winter was severe that year and spring slow to arrive. One cloudy cold day the cars began arriving at the Donaghadee manse, Barbara bounced out of a car and shook her head to tell me that the boy I rather liked hadn't come. I sagged with disappointment. Robert and some others spilled out of an old beige Hillman Minx and he came over to say hello. It was too cold and wet to face the beach as we had intended. Instead we picnicked in the manse dining-room and braved a walk around the harbour and lighthouse. We broke up into two and threes quite naturally along the footpath. I found myself walking with Robert and another girl. As we talked and joked time passed quickly. The fun accelerated at the harbour where time and again I found myself dragged to the edge and held over the precipice. I laughed a lot on that short walk, with the wind blowing our dripping ice-creams all over our clothes. I was discovering quickly what tremendous fun this guy was to be with; I had met few people with such wit and charm. I laughed that day till the tears ran down my cheeks. Robert slipped his arm gently around my shoulders and that of our companion, a strange tingle went down my spine, a rather pleasant feeling I thought. I think I fell in love with him that afternoon.

Time passed slowly that summer term – boarding school wasn't much fun and at best boring. I was leaning on my elbows at the library windows one grey day when a certain grubby beige Hillman Minx roared up College Gardens, caught my attention, and screeched to a halt at the side gate. A girl jumped out of the passenger seat, ran up the stone steps into McArthur Hall; the car turned, collected her as she ran out and was gone as quickly as it had arrived. I wandered up the oak panelled corridor towards the hall door trying to look unconcerned. On the hall table was a letter addressed to me . . .

> 'No doubt you will be surprised to receive this note, almost as surprised as I am to find myself writing it.
>
> Would it be possible to meet me for coffee sometime? Perhaps boarding poses difficulties . . . it might be that you may not want to make an arrangement of this nature. After all that, let me say that I would like, if at all possible, to have coffee with you on some suitable day.
>
> Kindest regards,
> Robert Bradford.

Sense told me not to reply too quickly, don't show yourself too keen, but I was bored and he was nice so he had his reply by the next post.

We sat in that old beige Hillman Minx XLF 368, at the front door of McArthur Hall. The roses in the circular bed

10

were just bursting into bloom. I couldn't get permission to get 'leave' as Robert's name was not on my parental list of suitable people with whom I could leave the premises. Sitting in the car was unheard-of cheek but not against any written law, and I could feel the indignant eyes from the staffroom window on the back of my neck. We talked of many things, finding more and more in common as time passed. The most important being that we both loved the Lord and were committed to serving him and the most surprising that we both felt drawn to missionary work in South America.

On our next date we met in the city centre, both in borrowed blue raincoats as we laughingly discovered. Life was taking on a beautiful new dimension. Waiting for that car arriving was fun. Now on the register as 'suitable' Robert could drive up to the door and collect me, though we both preferred the side gate where less people knew our business. Robert was always late and the car so caked with mud that it was rarely possible to read the number plate. Its soft leather bench seats, the gear stick on the steering column that Robert had to gently encourage to stay in place, the aroma of Old Spice that I still associated with that car, all combine in a feeling of nostalgia when I think of those carefree days. A careful driver, I thought. All the boys I knew with cars raced everywhere to impress their girlfriends, but not Robert. Having accidently injured a child in earlier years, and though not his fault, it had affected him deeply, so unless there was a reason for speed, he didn't use it.

My parents wanted to meet this boy and vet him for themselves. I was their last little fledgeling and they had no intention of allowing me to leave the nest early. One fateful day that July, Robert drove to our home in Donaghadee to be introduced. When I heard the car arrive I ran out to greet him. What a shock awaited me. Old XLF was sparkling in the sun. Robert was so different it took some getting used to. I hadn't seen this nervous, serious side before. He fixed his waves into place in the mirror for a third time with his ever faithful comb, straightened his suit, ran his finger inside his collar, and clearing his throat he said 'Right, throw me to the lions.' On the walk around the house to the wide mahogany front door, mischief bubbled over his apprehension and he stole a kiss or two. 'Serve you right if my Dad throws you out as a "queer" for wearing lipstick,' I teased as I remedied the situation.

It was a very tense meeting for me as my Dad and Robert tried quietly to score points off each other. Not liking to push too hard, Robert, I saw, bit a cheeky retort back as the mischief rose in his eyes on several occasions. The climax came almost at the end of a very quiet meal with stilted conversation when my Dad, who could contain his mischief no longer offered Robert a piece of cake. Robert replied 'I'm fine, thank you.' My Dad retorted 'I didn't ask you that, I said "Would you like some cake?" ' Robert swallowed hard and said quietly, 'No, thank you.' At that point I was ready to kill my Dad, who was enjoying every minute of it. He smiled at me, his blue eyes sparkling and I gave him a look fit to frizzle him, which almost made him laugh out loud. I can still hear myself shouting at him later, 'How could you be so mean?' He turned to look at me from his soft comfy favourite armchair with a look of complete innocence and said, 'Do, what dear?' The twitch at the corner of his eyes was not missed by me and I told him so, but I loved him so much that my anger didn't last long and we both ended up dissolving with laughter. 'Did you see his face when I offered the cake?' Dad chuckled. 'You are rotten!' I protested, laughing.

Our relationship was growing closer and we were spending more time together. Although this was my 'A' level GCE year I found it hard to settle to study. I shared a study room with a girl who worked very hard and always came out top, and she worried terribly about my leaning on my elbows in that turret room, gazing out over the tree tops in the direction of Edgehill College with my mind far from English, Geography, Biology or anything vaguely academic.

Our favourite place was a little café on the Ormeau Road called *The Gaslight*. Its dimly lit interior with high backed red leather tweed bench seats suited our mood, apart from the fact that a large slice of chocolate gateau and a mug of hot chocolate cost only 1s. 9d.

It was difficult to escape from school for many reasons; my father as a governor of the college always gave me a sense of responsibility and it wouldn't do his already badly damaged heart any good to be told his darling daughter was being expelled for breaking the rules. It seemed the stronger

12

sex were taboo in those days and only for a very understanding junior mistress who helped a lot could we have met as frequently as we did. It was wrong to talk to boy boarders. To be caught behind the bicycle sheds with one, however innocently, meant almost certain explusion. To have an outside boyfriend wasn't regarded as possible by the inmates but it was managed now and then. Concessions were creeping in through a few wise senior mistresses who had enough sense to see with the changing times that we needed to be allowed more freedom. The Duke of Edinburgh's Award Scheme was the first of these. To be allowed to walk out the gate in jeans, anoraks and knapsacks – what bliss – while those who hadn't the wit to join, wound their way along the pavements in navy napcoats, brimmed hats, courtshoes and in crocodile two by two, to various decidedly less exciting locations.

Somewhere along the line Robert's previous girlfriend had gained the nickname 'Big Scruff', not because of her state of dress or cleanliness, I might add, but purely as a term of endearment. When I came on the scene, being shorter and slighter than she was, I acquired the name 'Little Scruff'. I objected highly at first but fought a losing battle. I had never been all that keen on my own name, and at times almost had a complex about it as book after book, plays, films, etc, all cast 'baddies' as 'Norahs.' I was never the beautiful heroine who got the guy, always the sneaky murderess who ended up in jail. So changing my name wasn't as traumatic as it might have been. Next he started on my nose, 'I suppose the Lord had a purpose in giving you a bent nose, love; he made Gladys Alyward small to fit in with the Chinese; I haven't heard of them, but there is bound to be a South American Indian tribe with noses just like yours for us to go and minister to!' If he had survived till then it was because he had already ducked half way through. He was much too strong for me to continue the destruction of his waves. I would bide my time and get my own back at some opportune moment in the future.

The winter term of 1967 was very important in college for Robert and he took studying slightly more seriously which meant thinking about revising more than two days before exams. With very little effort Robert came top in most of his examinations and, humility not being his strong point, I ended up reminding him frequently of his enlarging head.

I discovered by accident that my Dad was marking some of Robert's exam papers, so I picked my time carefully one of the afternoons when I was at home and, cup of tea in hand, I sneaked quietly into Dad's book-lined study with its lovely sea view. The room was darkened by the overhead veranda outside, so for extra light a gold flecked anglepoise lamp lit the surface of the large oak roll-top desk at which the familiar silver-haired figure sat. His old Harris tweed jacket with leather patched elbows was worn into comfortable creases. On hearing me creep up he would swing around in his swivel chair, fountain pen poised in his immaculately manicured hand. He would smile over the glasses on the end of his large aquiline nose and covering the papers with his free hand he would put his pen between his teeth and take the cup of tea. 'They are all numbered sweetheart, he said, 'I couldn't tell you even if I wanted to!'

'I'll pick out his handwriting for you,' I said.

'No, love.' And he would nod towards the door . . . 'He's done well, as usual.' he threw over his shoulder as I reached the door. I ran back and hugged him, the fresh aroma of his aftershave mingling with the smell of his old jacket lingered in my nostrils as I planted a kiss on his broad fair-skinned forehead.

Robert and I became closer and closer, even writing to each other though living but a mile apart.

'There will be times when I shall surprise you, infuriate you, amuse you and enjoy doing all three, yet at the end of the day I want you to remember that I care deeply for you.'

My Aunt and Uncle had written to invite our family to Cork for a week in July and my parents thought it a lovely idea, although I was aware of something they didn't know. Some time before Robert had arranged to help on the Cork circuit for some of May and June.

XLF, that much loved and lamented car had been replaced by a suave blue and white Ford Anglia with pointed wings that looked better to the eye than it sounded to the ear. A rugby international in Dublin had seemed a lovely way to spend a Saturday in April. The atmosphere was spectacular and the game had a fair amount of action. Being with a

14

crowd of friends always enhances these occasions and this was no exception.

The journey home was unbelievable: the car behaved very badly, chugging its way along, then suddenly it would show a burst of speed, but eventually it settled to a high of about 17 mph. Every half hour Robert would stop and take off the large round filter and try to clean it. Then we would make a little better speed for a few more miles and gradually slow down again. On the fifth or sixth stop, I was watching through the gap of the upturned bonnet. Robert's frustration that had been at simmering point for a long time, boiled over. He kicked the radiator viciously, then calmly closed the bonnet yet again and got into the car. I stole a glance at him as he calmed himself, then offering a gentle chuckle I said 'Feel better?' Suddenly seeing the funny side of it, all tension was released and we collapsed in laughter. It seemed we couldn't remedy the situation, so we decided not to let it spoil our day, and I got a lovely letter of apology in the post soon after.

Preparing for 'A' level exams was to prove rather a stiff experience. I enjoyed Domestic Science and that made working for it easier. Biology was not in the same league. Cutting up mice that I had to catch and gas was rough enough, but when I found one had been pregnant and I had murdered five or six babies too, I lost all interest. Following and dissecting out the cranial nerves of a dogfish somehow lost any importance. I threw my project on house flies together, not even bothering to work out proper percentages on the figures. My entrance to nursing was arranged for September and not dependent on my exam results and so long as that was secure, I was unperturbed. English Literature I worked at as I was very fond of my teacher, affectionately known to us as Bilko. His likeness to the TV personality was undisputable, and his concern for his pupils and his love of teaching endeared him to us all. Robert's thoughtfulness became apparent when on the first day of my exams, I had a lovely note dropped in by hand.

When I'm sitting exams I somehow feel that two people are involved. This afternoon, love, three people will be involved – God, yourself and me – with a team like that how can things go wrong?!!!'

Robert was off to Cork again and we were back to letters as being our only form of communication. We quickly found in four days we could exchange two letters. His fine handwriting squeezed vast quantities on to one page, so four pages of his letters were equivalent to ten of someone else's. Having started out to drive the long journey to Cork he wrote he had made Cork easily by 6.45 pm that night.

Getting to know the West Cork folk was a delight for Robert. The beauty of the little country churches was not lost on him; he loved nothing better than to play the organ, conduct worship, preach and lead the singing with his melodious tenor voice, keeping the praise going at a spanking pace. Sometimes, the smaller the church the more at home he felt. The Cork folk warmed to this young man with so much energy, charm and wit and for him to be entertained by Youghal's equivalent to 'Mayor' was a big landmark in his life. '*By the way, I was almost arrested by the Garda on Saturday,*' he wrote. What could he have done now? I thought. '*I was stopped for having a faulty headlight.*' That *any* lights were working on that particular car amazed me!

'*After interrogation he said something like this to me, quote . . . Now oil tell yo what oil do witch ya!!! Oil take yore name but yo can forget it and it will be a name in de boke for me – Good Nought your Reverence . . . unquote.*'

Preaching was what Robert enjoyed most and he was getting plenty of practice. Getting to work with the young people of the circuit was also just up his street. His love of football meant carrying his boots with him everywhere as essential luggage; he was immediately accepted by the boys, and his charm got him accepted by the girls. He loved to talk of many things and answer questions, especially about his Lord, and his aim in life was to draw people closer to his Saviour.

My photo went with Robert to Cork and he reported back that our friends thought it rather good. '*I have told them not to expect too much because the photographer was very good at his job!*' He was very fortunate that he received any reply to that letter at all.

That God had chosen us for each other was becoming very real to us both. I believe nothing happens by chance and that the Lord allowed us that time apart to write to express what we really felt for each other. Robert had had a couple of close encounters before and had shied away at the last minute. He somehow seemed to feel trapped when marriage loomed large on the horizon. Why he should have wanted out of those 'tight corners' he didn't fully understand himself, but I learnt quickly not to pressurise him or I felt he would run a mile. Life with a Methodist minister offered little materially speaking, but that didn't seem important to me – if our union was ordained of God. The Lord had always provided for our family in a most amazing way; we never had money in the bank to talk of, but we never wanted for any good thing. I was convinced that the Lord who had provided so far wasn't going to stop now. So when he wrote in this vein Robert was careful to add, 'However I shall not say much more in this respect, for two reasons; firstly, I can imagine you sitting or rather hopping mad, secondly, I love you too much to risk convincing you that what I say is true.' For Robert to put that in writing was a big step. Again he would reiterate that our lives stretched ahead with so much time together.

My parents, by this time aware that Robert was in Cork, understood my keen encouragement over arrangements to stay in Cork ourselves. Robert's suggestion that I should stay on for a further weekend was dismissed as not possible. I wrote very despondently. 'But darling,' he replied 'we have lots of time, and more important still, infinite love for each other which will overcome any minor disappointments in our relationship.'

During my last two years at school, a petite little girl was 'boarded'. Though very young to be farmed out we soon discovered that her mum had died so she and her older brothers were all sent to school. A strange affinity grew between Jenny and me. On some of Robert's visits if I wasn't ready when he arrived at school, she would hop in the car and the two grew to like each other very much. She got very upset when he went to Cork so she wrote and told him so. I had to include her threatening letters in with mine. He wrote hastily back for her surname, thoughtfully surmising that she would love to receive her own mail. As the end of term came in sight, everyone started making plans for the holidays. Jenny began to crawl back into that protective shell I had spent the last years winkling her out of. I wrote of my concern for our special little friend and Robert advised, 'Don't worry too much – I know that isn't encouraging at the moment but Jenny probably realises very much how your departure will affect her and she is, in a sense, living it out in the present.'

It was Robert's birthday soon after and he had been working hard on Tom to be allowed time off to come North for a lightning visit. I was looking forward very much to seeing him again as it had seemed a lifetime since he had gone away. As time drew closer for us to meet, his letters became more compelling about our close relationship and I became very excited at the thought of seeing him again. Wednesday finally arrived and I rushed out to College Gardens for the few minutes we had at supper break. There he sat waiting, . . . it was so good to feel his loving arms around me. I felt so safe. I was free the next day to go home so we parted that night with the thought that it was only for a few hours. School on Thursday couldn't pass quickly enough, the hours simply dragged by. What should I wear? I changed my mind a dozen times. I finally decided on a pretty blue cotton dress and white cardigan.

We had a beautiful meal together and finally as the sun was setting, we drove towards Newtownards. The sky was ablaze with an orange flamed sunset. Scrabo Tower stood tall, silhouetted against the glorious sky. We drove up Scrabo Hill as far as the track would allow and got out to walk. The balmy breeze was brisker at the top of the hill and the view of Strangford Lough was as shimmering gold. Nowhere could be this beautiful, I thought. We walked hand in hand through the trees down the slope. I remember thinking, in years to come I won't remember the nettles or getting green lichen on my white cardigan from the trees. We talked quietly together and it seemed a natural progression to talk of permanent things.

'Will you marry me?' he murmured. 'We will never have much money, we will probably have to live in enormous draughty manses but I promise you life with me will always be different, it will never be dull or ordinary. I will make it fun.'

'Yes, I think I'd like that.' I replied.

On the slow drive home to Donaghadee I commented, 'How do you organise such beautiful sunsets every time we meet?'

'Don't you know I order them specially?' He smiled, pulling me closer along the bench car seat. 'I have a direct line,' he said pointing heavenward.

The time drew near for my family to go to Cork when my Dad's bad heart began to give us cause for concern. We all got together and discussed the forthcoming journey. Dad was obviously not fit for such a long journey so it was decided that rather than disappoint Dermot and me, and my Aunt and Uncle, Dermot and I should go on our own and share the driving.

The day finally dawned and we packed up Dermot's bottle green MG 1100. Mum and Dad prayed with us for 'journeying mercies'. Then we were off.

It was late when we piled into the house in Cork dragging our loaded suitcases to our bedrooms. I was upstairs and Dermot had been allocated to sleep in a glass conservatory off the breakfast room. The wooden shelves were filled with bright geraniums of pink and red, green ferns and other plants at various levels of growth. How lovely to sleep with such a beautiful aroma to wake to in the morning.

I asked to use the phone and contacted Robert. He was preaching in Youghal the next morning and had arranged for me to be included with him for lunch where he was being entertained. He would pick me up on his way through from Clonikilty about ten o'clock in the morning. I came off the phone bouncing. I explained the situation to my aunt and said I hoped she didn't mind if I wasn't back till tea time. Much to my surprise she was very hesitant but finally said I could go. I dressed quickly next day and at breakfast was given the shock news that my uncle had reversed the decision. I was not allowed to go! At nineteen I felt this kind of attitude very strange but found all pleading fell on deaf ears. The door bell rang, it was Robert and I explained I couldn't come. Robert's face whitened with fury and I had to watch a dejected figure walk out the gate he had just entered a moment before so differently.

Robert was preaching in the evening in Wesley Chapel in Cork and so nothing could be done to stop me seeing him there. He walked quietly up the steep steps to the pulpit with his sermon notes carefully tucked into his bible. Some rousing Wesley hymns set the tone for a lively time of worship, then I settled in the hard wooden pews to listen to what he had prepared. Not known even then for his brevity his fully written-out sermon covered ten to twelve large pages. By page four Robert was in full swing. He thumped the pulpit in his enthusiasm, his sheaf of white pages rose gently in the air and floated down in all directions to the carpeted floor below. The look of blind panic in Robert's white face as his sermon vanished made me want to die for him. He hesitated then gathered his train of thought and carried on as if nothing had happened. That was the last time he ever took anything other than brief notes to the pulpit. His preaching improved from that day. No longer was his head buried in the papers trying to read his notes; he learnt to rely more completely on his memory. He looked up more and became involved with his congregation.

Our time together for that short week was limited for two reasons. Robert had many duties on the circuit and my relations had arranged for Dermot and me to visit some friends and see some local sights. A midweek service was held in Huddersfield, the home of the Nicholson family. I had been told of this magnificent mansion from childhood, and at last I would see for myself. We drove up the long driveway that lovely evening, birds trilling in the trees as we passed through acres of woodland, rabbits scampering out of the way of the car. We had arrived, but what was this modern bungalow? Where was the large house? The upkeep of the building has become impossible we were told. So many repairs were needed and not practicable that the Nicholsons had decided to build a new home. The bungalow had been designed with a very spacious lounge to enable the Lord's work to be carried on there. Everyone crowded into this lovely home and were made to feel very welcome by that lovely Christian family. The thirty or so people settled in the rows of seats and the speaker was welcomed. The reading desk at which he stood was in front of a large picture window. The garden beyond was to be a grassy slope but was not yet cultivated. A mass of tall wild pink foxgloves covered the slope and made a magnificent background. Praising and worshipping the Lord in that setting was so easy. After supper and lots of chatting over old times, our hosts, discovering our interest in 'Huddersfield', offered to show us round the old house.

As we turned a bend in the road it came into sight. Its wide stone steps rose to a glass porch and inside its broad wooden door made me feel I was walking into a film set for *Gone with the Wind*. The gigantic key was turned in the lock and we walked into an enormous hall. The echoes of former grandeur were all around. Ornate ceilings, magnificent fireplaces, faded embossed wall hangings all gave a feeling of some lost age almost forgotten. The gently rising marble staircase supported solely by the wall, with its beautiful carved wooden bannister, made me expect any moment to see Scarlet O'Hara sliding down it, petticoats flying. A sad house I thought, gone were the laughter and life from within its walls.

A barbeque had been arranged by the young people. Dermot's sojourn each night in the draughty 'glass house' was taking its toll and by now he had developed a very nasty septic throat. 'If Dermot isn't going then I don't think you should' announced my aunt. So Dermot kindly dragged himself out for my sake and we met Robert there. We had been given a key to get in as my aunt and uncle didn't want to wait up for us. 'You really would almost think Norah came to Cork to see Robert and not us!' my aunt indignantly confided in Dermot before we left. It was drizzling intermittently by the time the fires were under way sufficiently to cook our sausages on sticks. Robert took me round with him and introduced me to some of the young people and I had my first taste of feeling an outcast. A young unattached minister is 'fair game' and a girlfriend coming on the scene is just not acceptable. I stuck very close to him that night feeling very isolated. Dermot, looking white and miserable, decided to go home early. We arranged that he would leave his window unfastened and I should get in that way later. The arrangement worked perfectly and no-one awoke. As abruptly as it began the week ended and we were packing up to go home.

Summer school week in August at Mourne Grange, Kilkeel was a time to be together again. The girls, leaders and visiting speakers and missionaries home on furlough occupied the main house, which was divided into many dorms, and rooms. Some boys slept in the basement gym while others slept in the monastery, a large white house at the end of the back lane which was the exit to the main road. Others in the 'Cabin' a small wooden, one storey structure with camp beds on the floor and any overspill into the sports pavilion that was dreaded as cold and damp with a hard concrete floor.

The day began with prayers and breakfast. At ten am we had an hour-long talk from the week's special speaker. You provided your own cushions for the wooden benches which grew harder as the week progressed, no matter how inspiring the speaker. Quiet time came next, after morning coffee. Then everyone split up on their own. A time to think over what had been said, to meditate, open the scriptures, talk quietly to the Lord and allow him to speak to you. As the days passed I could feel Robert drawing away from me. Was I clinging too much? I wanted to spend all possible time together, but he didn't seem to see it that way. Meals were very noisy occasions with two servers from each table balancing up to six plates of food in order to get their table fed first. The afternoons were free, and the grounds were laid out with a croquet lawn, two tennis courts and a football pitch. Sports tournaments were held and everyone joined in. It didn't matter how good you were; it was all very lighthearted until the semi-finals when things became serious. Robert was very good at most sports, tennis, cricket and football being his favourites. As one of those people with a permanent hole in their racket, I spent my time cheering him on. Cranfield beach wasn't far away and frequent visits were part of the week's highlights. The evening service would have a visiting missionary speaking and the light summer evenings culminated in most of us walking the couple of miles into Kilkeel where we would congregate in the local 'fish and chippy.'

Saturday night was 'Frivol night.' Each dorm had to produce a sketch and enact it for us all. Some were very professional and some not so good. Late that night after all the festivities I couldn't sleep. This week had not been as I expected and my mind was uneasy. Discipline was fairly lax and Barbara and I went out down the fire-escape for a moonlight walk and talk. Somewhere on our stroll we bumped into boys heading to the 'Cabin' to raid it. We naturally joined in; on one condition, they were not to disturb Robert as he had to leave early next morning for a service. In my white dress and Barbara in her white cardigan we were afraid we'd be picked out easily in the dark. Climbing in the open windows of the 'Cabin' we sat on the arms of an old armchair and watched mesmerised as silent shadows flitted through the small building turning over camp-bed after camp-bed. The only noise being that of the inmates as they grunted on hitting the floor with a thud. Some amazingly seemed to sleep on. At this point I discovered that this guy I'd fallen for was snoring! Gradually the spreadeagled forms began to gather their senses and the invaders began to flee as silently as they had come. Before we managed our own escape the light was thrown on by a bemused Robert. What a mess met his eyes. We stood drying the tears from our suppressed laughter, and still rocking and holding our sore sides we walked out leaving those poor guys scratching their heads in bewilderment. Final farewells were very difficult. We had made some very firm friends in that short week. Emotions ran high all round and many tears were shed.

We had a lift as far as Dundalk and that set us well on our way to Dublin. We got a bus the rest of the way where I stayed the week with my lovely aunt Lorna, and Robert was bunking down in a room of a friend at Trinity College. Each day together proved better than the one before. When there was just the two of us everything seemed fine. Perhaps I had exaggerated the sinking feeling I had experienced a week before. The weather was glorious and much warmer than the exposed Kilkeel. We visited Cathedrals and other sights.

We planned a picnic to the seaside the next day. I was preparing it when Robert arrived with a borrowed car. We had a beautiful time together and enjoyed the picnic. While walking up the steep sloped road near the shore, the wind having proved too cold, we came upon a small restaurant. The notice in the window advertised 'Gold Medal for Wheaten Bread, First Prize for Wheaten Scones.' We went in expectantly and ordered a pot of tea and some scones. The little old lady fussed around and went off to fetch the tea. Robert spied the actual certificates on the walls. In bold print, '1935 Gold Medal for Wheaten Bread,' '1937 1st Prize for Wheaten Scones.' 'Do you think we will get the prize-winning entries?' Robert suggested.

September 1967 began with my plunge into the nursing world at the Royal Victoria Hospital, and Robert's last year in College. We filled our days with laughter, joking and having fun. With a lot of persuasion, Robert agreed to attend the nurses 'formal' dance in December. With my meagre salary of ten pounds a month I couldn't buy a long dress so I set to making one. The big night came and looking fantastic in his hired tuxedo, Robert arrived and we nervously set off the the ballroom. We spent the evening tramping on each other's toes and apologising. Not a memorable time we decided. Dancing wasn't going to be our greatest achievement. Perhaps God was showing us which directions were wrong. The New Year was to be spent apart, much to our disappointment, but it was some consolation that it was for the Lord. Robert and some other students were to take a mission in Castlederg.

'*Do you know that your name has infiltrated even to Co Fermanagh?*' he wrote. *Not only that but also the fact that I was at a dance with a very glamorous girl. So my name is mud!*' He had discovered, having visited some friends in nearby Fivemiletown. '*Norah, my love, the bell has just sounded to greet the New Year. My thoughts and love are yours completely not only tonight but for ever. Write soon and keep your eyes off those medics. Don't work too hard my love, and do take care for I cannot do without your love and inspiration.*'

The first draft of stations came out in the new year with Robert set for 'Cregagh'. A very lively large city church and we were both excited. When the next stationing said the same we decided to pay an *incognito* visit to the said church, ie without clerical collar. Our impression was not exactly favourable but filled with enthusiasm to change the whole world, changing things at 'Cregagh' was going to be 'no problem' to Robert.

My off-duty didn't allow me to be present at Robert's inauguration at Cregagh. He picked me up at the hospital later bubbling with enthusiasm. 'The people are lovely and that church has tremendous potential. If I can get the leaders' backing I could do so much for the young people there.'

Being on circuit again, being able to put into practice the training of the previous four years plus many of his own ideas, was a delight for Robert. Although the opportunity to preach didn't present itself often, Robert found plenty of outlets for his enthusiasm. Becoming involved in the church football team was not solely for his love of the game and keeping fit, but as an avenue to the hearts and confidence of

the young people. As more boys were drawn into the life of
the church through football it was easy to draw in the girls.
Robert wanted to provide facilities to encourage these
young folk, so he persuaded the leader's board to allow him
to use an upstairs hall for an after church coffee bar. 'The
After Eight Club' was born. Robert went to a lot of trouble
to book Christian groups to sing and organise special speakers from many walks of life, to really encourage lively discussion on many Christian and moral topics, always insist-
ing that the young people gave their full attention for a short
time for him to talk of what was closest to his heart.

As time progressed we seemed to grow apart. During the
next twelve months we had many upsets. Several times we
parted, tried other relationships but seemed to drift
together again. My father, who had been having heart
attacks since before I was born, refused to be an invalid and
continued with his committees and other duties when he felt
at all able and even when he wasn't. On their way to Church
Conference in Dublin in June 1969 my parents broke their
journey at Portadown to stay the week-end with my brother
and his family. On Monday a massive coronary took my
darling Dad from this world into the welcoming arms of his
Saviour. I was off duty between two and five pm that day
and intended to go down town but something held me back
from leaving the building. A phone call from an assistant
matron broke the shocking news to me. I phoned Robert
and my friend Barbara. She and her father rushed over and
stayed until Robert arrived to transport me to Portadown.
This traumatic period of my life was used by God to draw
Robert and me together again in a way that finally led to our
decision to become engaged six months later. I had nine
months' training still to do and Robert was to be ordained in
June. My mother was rather anxious that we should not
marry until I had done my final exams, a condition to which
we agreed. My 'finals' were to be in September so we set the
date for our marriage for December, 1970.

We now began to think seriously of missionary work and
we made tentative enquiries with the thought of going
abroad the next year. That would give us time for Robert's
ordination in June, for me to finish my exams, and for us to
be married.

The stationing committee in their wisdom had placed

Robert in Suffolk Church. Neither of us had much idea where it was; we had some vague idea that it was on the outskirts of Belfast. After quick investigation we found it. We were rather excited by the fact that we weren't to be parted. We had expected that Robert would be shipped off to some inaccessible corner of Ireland after June. But here he was to stay within easy reach of the 'Royal' Hospital, where I worked.

We discovered through the undercurrents of the Methodist grapevine that the Suffolk people were not too pleased at Robert's appointment. They hadn't had any continuity of ministry, having had several short-stay ministers. They pleaded that they needed an older, experienced man who could given them a good, steady ministry to pull them together. They certainly didn't want another man who would be leaving in a year's time to go to the mission field. Understanding their feelings, we prayed about what we should do. We felt that it was right for us to go to Suffolk, so we offered a promise that we would not go abroad for five years.

Robert's ordination in June in front of a packed Grosvenor Hall was a moving occasion. Robert spoke on 'Putting love first' in the Christian life. July came, and instead of heading for Suffolk for Robert's debut I found myself being wheeled on a trolley towards a surgical ward in preparation for removing my inflamed appendix. When I finally was back on my feet some weeks later I found I would not be able to take my finals. I would however be allowed to leave the hospital in November having served my allotted time and take my finals externally.

Wedding preparations were well in hand. Finally the invitations were sent out, wedding presents began to pour in. The flowers were ordered. One night I had an awful nightmare about the wedding. I was standing in the church vestibule ready to enter the church on my brother's arm when I discovered I had forgotten my bouquet. I grabbed a bunch of chrysanthema from a nearby vase. The stench that hit my nostrils was one that only people who have removed stagnant water from a forgotten chrysanthemum vase can know. The green water was dripping all over my beautiful dress; at that point I woke up in a cold sweat, so thankful it had only been a dream.

I was standing in the hall of my home in Donaghadee in my long white wedding gown with shoulder length train, headdress and veil in place. The bridesmaids in their long lemon dresses had left in the limousine along with Mum and my sister. My sister burst back into the house.

'We forgot the bouquets,' she shouted as she rushed to fetch the sprays of anemones from the cool outhouse.

'Don't take too much heed of dreams, do you' I crossly scolded myself. For I had been standing without my own bouquet of lemon and white roses quite ready to step into the car.

The heater was not working and a rug was wrapped round me. I was so afraid of crushing my dress that I unwrapped it as soon as our journey to Belfast began, preferring to freeze. When we got to Bradshaw's Brae the car was crawling along.

'What's the hold up?' my brother Brian enquired.

'Don't want to be early,' came the reply.

'I would prefer to go twice round the block when we get there,' I said, afraid we'd hit traffic jams. We did and arrived a good ten minutes late. By the time photographs were taken and I was walking up the aisle I was twenty minutes late. Robert was standing at the communion rail as the Wedding March from the Sound of Music sounded out. He turned slightly as I came level and, looking very strained, gave me a weak smile.

'This guy isn't sure,' I thought . . . 'It's normal to be nervous,' I rationalised, 'he's had a lot to organise, probably hasn't slept too well.'

'How well do I really know this man?' I wondered.

2

Torrential rain poured out of the black sky that April day in 1943 making the deaconess's journey through the muddy cobbled Belfast streets almost impossible. Soaked through she stepped off her bike at Grove Street. 'What number had the NSPCC given her?' She checked her note and knocked at No 9. No answer. She tried again, and then a neighbour across the road shouted, 'She's upstairs in bed, Go on in!'

Pushing the front door open she stepped into the dark hall, she looked up. There on the stairs was a small bare legged boy scrubbing down the wooden staircase. Into the upstairs bedroom were crowded five children, looking helplessly at their very thin, haggard mother in the bed. Mrs Bradford lay gasping, ashen faced, almost at death's door it seemed to the deaconess. On top of the mother lay the smallest child, obviously very ill also. Ushering the children out, the deaconess did her best to make the woman more comfortable. The war years were not easy on anyone, but this family were suffering more than most it seemed.

Cycling back to the Mission, thoughts raced through her head. These children didn't need a holiday as she'd been told, they needed much more. The ministers quickly came to the decision that if the mother could be persuaded to part with them, the children should be taken into *Childhaven*, an orphanage attached to the mission, that is, all except the baby who at barely two years was too small. The children were taken to the Co-op with clothes vouchers and essential items were bought. How thrilled those children were to go shopping! Gradually, as Mrs Bradford realised that these people really cared, her story unfolded.

Her husband had a milk business in Donegal Pass where they had all lived. As war progressed and life in Belfast became dangerous with the blitz, Mrs Bradford and her six children were evacuated to Limavady. By this time she was expecting her seventh child. On the 8th June, 1941 a baby boy was born to the Bradfords. His mother named him *Robert Jonathan*.

By the time the mother was out of hospital with the baby, Mr Bradford, she discovered, had sold up the milk business

and vanished. Without a penny in the world and seven
children to feed she had to set herself to find a home. No 9
Grove Street, near York Road became that home. She
moved herself and her children from Ballykelly, Limavady
back to Belfast. Things went from bad to worse. Her health,
which had never been good, deteriorated. Hospitalisation
became necessary and in the autumn of 1942 the children
were again evacuated, this time to Ballymoney. When at last
she was out of hospital, Mrs Bradford came to fetch them.

Short sojourns in hospital were not enough to cure the
turberculosis that had now been diagnosed. The children
tried to help around the house but their mother's strength
was waxing dim. Gradually bronchial pneumonia developed
on top of the TB. The deaconess arrived and Mrs Bradford
was taken into Whiteabbey Hospital, Robert was collected
by Mr and Mrs Nicholson to stay with them indefinitely,
and his brothers and sisters, in new clothes, were off to
Childhaven orphanage and a new life.

40 Hunter Street was Robert's new home and it was to
remain so for a long time. A tiny two-up, two-down house,
as they were affectionately known, no different in size from
the one he had left, except – he had a whole bedroom to
himself. This took some getting used to. Times were hard
for everyone but everything the Nicholsons had was
lavished on Robert, their foster child. He had new clothes
when no-one else could get them. Dinky cars till they came
out his ears. Life was brightening for this perky, fair,
curly-haired two year-old. His cheeky smile won the hearts
of many of the neighbours. Mrs Nicholson worked in Grosvenor Hall, Belfast Central Mission until lunch time and
Robert was sent to a day care centre until his new mum got
home. He was miserably unhappy about this and left
everyone in no doubt as to his feelings. A relation of the
Nicholsons was housebound in 43 Hunter Street and Uncle
Bob, as Robert called him, offered to take Robert during
the mornings. This arrangement suited everyone and
Robert grew to love Uncle Bob and Aunt Liz, his sister.
Aunt Lizzy Bell worked in a local laundry as an inspector
and mender. Uncle Bob has been unable to come out of No
43 since his father had died, a phobia which he only managed to overcome on rare occasions when he thought Robert
was being hit or had hurt himself. Aunt Liz worked long

hours for very small pay, as did most working-class folk in those days.

While the Nicholsons were at work Aunt Liz and Uncle Bob gently guided Robert along and he spent more and more time in No 43. Their tremendous sense of humour and fun gave Robert an insatiable appetite for jokes as he grew. There were plenty of playmates in those narrow streets with rows of terraced houses crammed back to back. The rooms were so small there wasn't even space to 'swing a cat'. Row upon row of red brick houses in street upon street of terraces stretched in all directions off the Donegall Road and Sandy Row, in the area Robert now knew as home; individuals ritually painted their homes freshly every year in time for the 12th July celebrations. Though small, the majority of the homes were immaculately clean and well furnished. No 40 Hunter Street was no exception with its neat back yard and outside privy. When very young Robert showed his aptitude for football, and the tiny ones playing in the street were no bother to the residents. Traffic was infrequent and sometimes took the form of the rag-man's horse and cart. His piercing cry brough the children running from their homes. For a bundle of rags the children were given a colourful balloon.

'What colour do you want?' the rag-man enquired.

'Blue, please' said Robert. 'I like blue.'

The ricketty cart bumped off again over the cobbled streets with its load of faded, worn, rejected clothes and gay, floating balloons, one in sharp contrast to the other. Further down the street the old horse stood patiently still again at his master's bidding. The bones were beginning to protrude through his thick hide. Hanging his head as he rested from his weary travelling, yet again, he watched the children scamper around him, swinging on their makeshift swing tied to a lamp-post, playing 'marlies' with their coloured glass marbles on the pavement.

When Robert was of school age Blythe Street Primary School was just around the corner. School, to Robert, was a place to gather a football team together, not a place for serious study. Break-time and lunch-time were the important times, the rest of the day was to be got through as quickly and with as little effort as possible.

Church on Sundays with the Nicholsons was at Gros-

30

venor Hall, Belfast Central Mission. The large hall and gallery were packed for those services where the rousing hymns of the Wesleys were sung with a fervour that almost lifted the roof. Attending Sunday school there and at a local Presbyterian church, Robert found his knowledge of the Bible expanded – when he listened! In the evening at the 'hall' a meal was prepared in the smaller back hall for 'down and out' tramps. They would filter in through the Glengall Street door and be given a hot meal. This practical Christianity impressed Robert. Time was then taken to speak to those poor creatures that the world had written off. In their rags and tatters, their several coats tied together with string, their boots with gaping soles and their unsavoury odours, they looked with tired eyes to the platform where beautifully dressed young people with the light of Jesus in their eyes would sing of their Lord. Someone would tell of a Savour whose love is for all, no matter how humble, no matter what they had done or not done, a Saviour who was waiting with open arms for them. They only had to open the door of their heart to experience an unspeakable joy. Slowly as time grew near for the evening service, one by one the tramps, male and female, would gather their possessions, their precious bundles of newspapers and rags to keep out the cold, damp, dark night, and go out to face another week of life in doorways and alleys or doss houses or wherever they found shelter. One tramp, however, would turn and make his way into the great hall for the service. He usually sat about three rows in front of Robert and the Nicholsons. As the time for the service drew near a beautiful child with blond curly hair would trip in the main Grosvenor Road entrance, her pretty clothes flouncing as she pranced her way down the several aisles to sit beside the tramp. Robert reckoned she was almost the same age as himself. He many times wondered about his own Dad, Was that what he was like now? He had only met him once; he had come to the house just after he had moved in with the Nicholsons, patted him on the head, given him sixpence and gone again. His sense of painful rejection welled up within him, but he fought it back down.

Robert's teacher began to take an interest in him at school and persuaded the Nicholsons to send him to elocution and music lessons. Mr Nicholson, who himself played a pedal organ and accordion, made sure Robert practised at least one hour every night. His music teacher was impressed with his ability but felt a piano would give him a better grounding than the organ, so the Nicholsons managed to purchase a piano. Primitive Street Methodist Church Boys' Life Brigade was just round the corner and Robert started to go there. Lots of the local kids went and the care and discipline did them a lot of good. But Robert discovered quickly that if he got himself thrown out he could play football, so he would be disruptive just enough for him and some friends to get thrown out and then have some football fun outside. For all that, the Boys' Brigade had a profound influence on his life. The Christian discipline taught there wasn't wasted on him, though the officers might have thought so at the time.

The narrow streets hardly gave room for football and occasionally windows got broken if boys got too enthusiastic. One such day a fast match was in progress. Goals were being scored with enthusiasm. Robert got the ball, dribbled it up the potholed street, kicked with all his might and scored.

Cheers went up from the boys, but Robert looked far from happy. While the ball might have gone through the appropriate goal posts, Robert's grubby shoe had gone in another direction completely and the ominous sound of tinkling glass left the boys scattering in all directions. Robert owned up to his misdemeanour as he couldn't have explained away his lost shoe. He got off with a reprimand and paid for the window. Football was frowned on by a lot of the residents for that very reason, so it was better to play a few streets from home. Then if the police chased you, you might not be so easily identified. Gafikkin Street and the other streets beside the trolley-bus depot were a favourite with Robert and his mates. With the dug-out base for tram inspection there were numerous places to hide if in danger of being chased.

Football took up every spare minute of Robert's life and led him and his mates through the elite Malone Road to the wide open spaces of Barnetts Park. There they thought they could play their cricket and football without annoying anyone, but it was not to be. The local residents complained about the boys and the police came. They quietly watched the boys and could see no problem but took their names and addresses anyway. Reporting back to their superiors they were overruled and letters were sent to the boys to tell them they were not allowed to continue their outings. Something deep inside Robert told him *Some day I'll live up here myself, some day I will.'*

The eleven-plus exam loomed in front of Robert, but as few of the children expected to get it and it was considered an unexpected bonus if some passed, no great emphasis was placed on it. Robert failed, though he had worked for it.

Just at that time an evangelistic mission was organised in Grosvenor Hall at which the famous W E Sangster was to preach. The spacious hall and gallery filled to bursting point every night. Robert and his mates went along. The singing was thrilling and the strange English accent of the great man of God made for compelling listening. Robert's pulse quickened as he listened night after night. Though only eleven he realised that the appeal for people to commit their lives to Christ also meant him. He wasn't doing anything terribly wrong, but his life had no goal beyond football posts. He began to walk forward, he had to be up at the front. He needed Christ in his heart, guiding his life. *Lord Jesus, come into my heart,'* he quoted in prayer as he knelt. *'Come in to stay, come in today, Lord Jesus come into my heart.'* And he did.

A long battle lay ahead for him as his relationship with his Lord built up over the years. His next four years were spent in Linfield Secondary Intermediate School which adjoined the Blythe Street Primary. He tried to work steadily and well, he was working now for his Lord and he made the 'A' class each year.

Playing football for his Boys Brigade team was a big part of his life. He was good and his mates began to depend on him. He liked people depending on him, even the Nicholsons had begun to depend on him a lot. One Saturday on a very rough football pitch, Robert sliced his left knee badly. Blood pouring from the injury, he was taken to a nearby hospital. It was duly stitched and he was sent home. Within a few days it was 'up like a bap'. Going this time to a different hospital he was informed it mustn't have been cleaned out properly before being stitched. They removed some stitches and drained some pus. Again he was dispatched home. Sitting on the sidelines during matches was not his style and he found it very hard to sit still, but the pain from his knee reminded him when he got too enthusiastic. While watching the match a skirmish developed near him. Without time to escape, he found four muddy bodies descending on him, all fighting for the ball. A stray foot caught Robert full on his injured knee. The whole wound split open and green pus flew in all directions. Rolling around on the ground in abject agony, fighting back the tears that welled up, he bit into his lip hard. The wounded knee was more carefully dealt with this time and healed quickly. Apart from his knee cap being at an obscure angle and a nasty scar, he had no further trouble from it.

Uncle Bob Bell's health was deteriorating. The leg ulcers he had had for many years drained his health. Finally he died and was laid to rest in Belfast City Cemetery.

Elocution had given Robert a good speaking voice. He was losing his broad Belfast accent, saying 'ing' instead of the usual 'in' at the end of words, and many of his playmates didn't like it. They felt with the voice there had to be snobbery also and they had no room for that. He had to stick a lot of ragging from the other kids and a certain unpopularity because of it.

School days were soon over. With two letters of reference, he set off at fifteen in search of his fortune. He applied for a job advertised by a window blind company, to work in their shop but soon found he didn't like it. He moved on to a job in King Street with a wholesale shirt manufacturers and settled in better. He was given responsibility for cycling around the city on various errands which he thoroughly enjoyed. Meanwhile he was playing football for Glenavon Football Club on Saturdays as an under-eighteen. One very special Saturday he made sure his kit was spanking clean. He had new laces for his boots, he checked his studs to see if any need replacing, he even replaced last week's mud with some polish. The game was in full swing when he had sorted out who was who from the audience. He knew the local Belfast team officials, so by a process of elimination he figured out who the Sheffield Wednesday's man was. He really made that round piece of muddy leather move as he dug up the green turf with his ferociously flying feet. He put everything he had into the game that day as the sweat soaked into his team shirt. He leapt in the air punching it with his fist when he got the offer of a month's trial with Sheffield Wednesday's under-eighteen team. They could get him digs in Sheffield, they added, if he gave them his answer soon.

'Bobby', as he was known in football circles, was packed and off like a shot on the first possible boat. His digs were to be in the home of Mr Springit, the professional goalkeeper with the Sheffield Wednesday team. His excitement was hardly bearable as he walked into the stadium that first morning for training. He had met the other lads in the changing room; they were a motley bunch but seemed nice on the whole. He was really going to work at this. This was now to be his whole life. He soon found he had a lot of time on his hands. The other lads enjoyed going to the cinema but Robert soon tired of their ideas of fun. Football was now a way of life for him, just what he's always wanted . . . or was it? Harry Catterick ear-marked him for a good career in the English League but even that didn't quell all his doubts. Sheffield Wednesday offered him an amateur status contract because he was slight in build with a weight-lifting programme thrown in. He just wasn't happy! He began to think if he went home he could have his own friends around him and still play football at week-ends and in the evenings. Possibly a superior arrangement. Coming off the pitch one night after an exhausting game a man in the crowd leaned forward and pushed a piece of paper into his hand. When he sat down muddy and tired in the changing room he uncrumpled it. It was a tract. As he read it he realised his life was no longer Christ-centred: football was fun but he was wasting his days away. He could see that when it got to the big league and he was of drinking age it would be all 'booze, girls and riotous living'. That finally made up his mind. He came home rather quieter and wiser than he had gone away.

Now an apprentice for a firm in Fountainville Avenue which put spectacle frames together, Robert signed up again for Glenavon Football Club and travelled to Lurgan for training and games. After a while he found even this became tedious. It left little time for his enlarging social activities. So he arranged a transfer to Distillery, which was closer to home.

The Grosvenor Hall had a lively group of about thirty teenagers, most of whom attended the Friday night Youth Club, Sunday night after church Fellowship and Tuesday night Christian Endeavour. These friends and activities made a big difference to Robert. He had been verging on a razor edge for some time as to whether he chucked in this whole Christianity business and did the things that gave immediate pleasure, or chose the other path that, it seemed, needed a certain amount of restraint and discipline but he knew would give a lasting peace that was much more worthwhile. He found the friendship and fellowship of other young Christians, struggling with the same problems he had, very refreshing.

Robert's life had turned a corner. He had come through the blind panic of those teenage years, chosen a path that was leading him to a closer relationship with his Lord. In No 40 'Wee Jimmy' as he called his foster dad, had had some difficulty keeping control over him. Robert regarded himself, like all eighteen year-olds, as possessor of all knowledge. 'Wee Jimmy', who was four foot nothing (according to Robert!) had muscles of iron. On one of these fracas he took Robert, all of five foot nine, by the scruff of the neck, lifted him up till he couldn't touch the ground with his feet and told him exactly what he thought of him. The deep humiliation felt by Robert at this episode lived to stop him in his tracks many times in case he should re-live it.

'Wee Jimmy' and Sadie Nicholson had to be up for Jimmy's early shift at the shipyard, so they were nearly always in bed by ten o'clock at night. Robert loved coming home to an empty kitchen and scullery. Making himself some large white bread and bacon butties, he would settle himself with a large pot of tea at his elbow in an easy chair and just enjoy the quiet. This was the time of the day he found it easiest to have a talk with God. He would place an empty chair in front of himself and just chat – tell Jesus of the day's happenings, ask forgiveness for his shortcomings, for the harsh word said in temper, for the thoughtless deed done in haste. A beautiful peace was taking over his life. He had a gentle, gracious girlfriend who meant the world to him, and had had a long discussion with his boss and minister as regards his future.

One evening he was praying in his quiet time when a strange awe gripped him. The whole house became still and silent as if a mighty hand was resting on it. The presence of the Lord was all around. Robert covered his head with his hands and silently knelt, hardly daring to breathe in case he should disturb the stillness. For hours he stayed motionless drinking in the unspeakable joy that seemed to be all around. He finally arose, went to bed and slept like a baby. The next morning, the sky was a more radiant blue than ever, the birds sang more lustily as if they had been party to the previous night's experience. He dressed quickly, bounded down the narrow wooden staircase, threw his arms around Sadie, who shrank away in fright at his exuberance. He was into work early with full knowledge of where his future lay. His boss, a lovely Christian man, gave him all the encouragement and support he possibly could. Rev Eric Gallagher, Robert's minister, was overjoyed at his news. He personally took Robert under his wing. He would have to have GCE 'O' levels and local preacher exams to gain entrance to Edgehill Theological College, the Methodist training centre for Ireland. '*So I'm to be a minister*,' Robert thought.

Night classes in Shaftesbury House School solved the first problem of how to get GCE exams. Finding the hard slog of study now quite enjoyable, he discovered he had perhaps been a late starter and in fact he could attain quite high marks. Local preacher's exams were the next hurdle. Greek and Hebrew were a new experience. Languages took time and much slog as whole new alphabets and vocabularies had to be learnt, but Robert was determined.

College was not grant-aided so he would need extra money. 'Wee Jimmy' and Sadie were very generous but Robert felt a better job would help him save more. A position was advertised in the local press for a clerk in Ewart's Spinning Mill American department. Robert applied and got the post. He was to take over from a chap called Ken and they were given a few days together for Ken to show Robert the ropes. Robert was quick to learn, and they found they had much in common to chat about. Quickly becoming firm friends Robert listened to his friend's animated conversation. Robert felt that Ken had a God-given insight into the Bible that was refreshing and rare. As he talked Ken leafed through his ever present well-worn *Phillips* volume of the New Testament expounding what the Lord had revealed to him. British Israel truth was new to Robert. The days together passed quickly but the friendship what had started so amazingly was to last a long time.

Ewart's Mill was completely different from anywhere Robert had worked to date. Perhaps it was that his life now had real purpose, a really worthwhile goal. He was now aware that he had potential, aware that his elocution and musical training had all been in God's plan. Perhaps this made him walk a little taller than before. His identity was emerging with this new-found confidence.

The corner where Sandy Row and Donegall Road met was not far from Hunter Street, and was a favourite meeting place for some of the local lay-abouts. On one particular sunny day Robert was walking past when a well-known harmless creature accosted him by the arm. 'Bradford, any odds?' Meaning it would be wise to hand over his loose change. Robert put his hand in his pocket, unabashed at the seeming threat and handed over a half-crown and some pennies.

'Is that it?' said the man.

'That's it Sammy,' Robert walked away smiling.

Robert worked hard and by March 1964 he had finished his local preacher's exams and been accepted by the Methodist Church in Ireland to enter their ministerial training course. He also wanted to work for a degree so he had contacted Wolsey Hall, Oxford to do a Diploma correspondence course.

With all these new horizons ahead, Robert began to question the relationship with his girlfriend and finally extracated himself from it. For his first year the Methodist Conference had decreed Robert should be placed on circuit, so now he had to purchase a black suit and a clerical collar or two before he was off to the Fermanagh/Tyrone border, to a little place called Fivemiletown.

The big day had almost arrived when he was walking down Sandy Row in his new gear, feeling a new sense of responsibility on his shoulders, along with his clerical collar, and perhaps showing off just a little, when he was again accosted by 'Sammy'. There was a very marked difference in his attitude though. He didn't grab Robert by the arm as before, or even block his way. He siddled up alongside him as he walked.

'Good-day Mr Bradford,' he said, touching his cap respectfully.

'Mr Bradford it is now,' thought Robert, chuckling inwardly, trying not to smile.

'Would it please your Reverence to help a poor fellow human being less fortunate than yourself, Sir?'

Robert smiling widely by now, handed over the usual change and went his way chuckling loudly. He loved those working class people. 'Salt of God's earth' he called them, 'There's no time for nonsense in those homes,' he would say, 'No airs or graces'. For most folk there was no escape, the street they spent their childhood in was where they spent their married life and where they died. Few ever had the chance Robert was getting and he not only knew it but was especially grateful for it.

'Fermanagh, here I come,' he thought as he packed. He was off to be a 'fisher of men.' He knew he was fully in the Master's will and the sense of peace that gave him was only superseded by the excitement of what lay ahead. Any tensions he felt he bottled up as usual. The traumatic effect of his early rejection had left him still inwardly very insecure but he pushed any fears to the back of his mind: he *had* to trust in his Lord. He was now stepping out in faith, in total dependence on a God who had never let him down.

Perhaps if the inhabitants of Fivemiletown had known a little about the human being that was about to be unleashed on them they would have taken more notice. Rev Bolster took him to the farm where he was to stay and introduced him to the people he was to be with. Robert felt instantly at home and it wasn't long before he had his shoes off and his feet planted firmly on the large Aga stove, enjoying its gentle heat. All sorts of goodies were soon produced and Robert had his introduction to a farmhouse fry as only country folk know how to make. The cosy farmhouse kitchen had a charm all of its own with its well worn comfy chairs and sleeping mongrel dog. The aroma of hot baked wheaten bread, the taste of warm frothy milk straight from the cow, a fry of griddle wheaten, soda bread, potato bread, fresh eggs and bacon were tastes he acquired a liking for remarkably quickly. The pungent aroma of farm animals in close proximity he found took longer to get used to. The picture of washed down concrete yards and hosed down milk biers, large waving fields of ripening corn and barley with winding, bumpy lanes leading from farm to farm, were such a complete contrast to anything he had ever known at Hunter Street.

The local football team came in delegation to ask for his

help. They mentioned gingerly the fact that they changed in the local pub, expecting a prompt refusal, but Robert said that wouldn't matter, he wouldn't be going there to drink. Fivemiletownians didn't quite feel the same. Rumour soon had it that the new assistant minister had been seen going in and out of the 'local'. It took a long while for the old 'diehards' of the community to understand, but Robert stood his ground; through football maybe he could gain some souls for the Lord. Many of these men had never darkened a church door.

Writing home meant frequent trips to the local post-office and the realisation that the Fermanagh girls, and one girl in particular, were very charming. He was rather lonely and a few outings ensued. After a very pleasant evening out Robert set off to walk back to the farm. A heavy fog descended with the dark and what should have been a very enjoyable stroll down a country road turned into a nightmare. The absolute blackness of that country night was eerily exaggerated by the fog and a cow mooing close by. No street lights, few sounds and now no way of seeing more than a few yards in front. The centre white line seemed the only way of finding his way. This worked fine until a car rounded the corner and Robert had to scramble into the ditch. Having cleaned the muck off his feet on the grass verge as he pulled himself out of the 'shuck' he again found the while line. He hadn't far to go so it wouldn't be long before the lane came in sight. It was a long time later, when he saw town lights glimmering hazily in the fog in the distance. Could he have missed the lane and walked the many miles to the next town? Surely not! He looked around for familiar landmarks. By now the fog had lifted sufficiently for him to distinguish the countryside and realise he had somehow managed to do a complete about turn and had walked right back into town. Eventually he reached the farm tired out but relieved, sank into a comfy chair and happily stroked their friendly little dog.

A previous assistant minister with musical ability had started a small choir in the area. The next assistant encouraged and nurtured them and Robert in turn with his expertise on the piano and love for good gospel music took them under his wing. Their fame spread and invitations to sing began to flow in. Packed into two or three bone-rattling cars they would wind their merry way along the lanes to their allotted assignment. Always leaving at the last minute they had to travel rather fast: upon rounding a corner Robert was just in time to see the lead car drive over the ditch instead of taking a bend. Robert stopped quickly and everyone ran to the hedge just as the car came to rest on its side. The door flung open as if it were a submarine hatch and a large head popped up followed by an equally large body. Pushing his three hairs back into place across his bald pate, the man replaced his cap and reached down to help his passengers out.

'What happened, John?' Robert shouted anxiously from the road. John looked up nonchalantly at his friend.

'I think . . . I ran out of road,' he said hesitantly in his thick Fermanagh accent and with a slow grin stealing over his face. A local farmer was engaged to tow the car back on to the road with his tractor and soon they were on their way again without any obvious ill-effects, except a slightly more battered car.

The small churches on the circuit were sometimes far apart and fairly sparsely attended and there were often as many as five different services on one Sunday. The tiny stone buildings were generally heated by a central coke boiler and first into church got the warmest seats.

Soon after his arrival, Mr Bolster had given Robert the job of transporting a special visiting preacher around. Robert quickly got the impression that this preacher thought more of his own preaching ability than did the Fermanagh people. The third service was after lunch. The farmers had been up very early as usual that morning to tend to their cows and other livestock, and as the service progressed the effects of their large Sunday lunch combined with the heat set up by the coke boiler settled some of them into a gentle doze. The minister was plodding through his sermon when a snorting sound reached his ears. Looking down to find the culprit he spied the offending party. Pointing at the farmer with an indignant finger he roared at his neighbour,

'Wake that man up!' Without even unfolding his arms the neighbour said,

'Yud best come down and do that yursel, twer you that put him to sleep.'

Robert hid his face in a hymn book, and smothering his laughter, managed to last out the service.

Setting off on one of his first visits with enthusiasm, he marched up to a house and proudly knocked on the door. A young girl, her bright ginger hair in rollers, opened it. With dismay she saw the clerical collar, panicked and slammed the door in his face. Her rather redfaced mother opened it again to find Robert wondering quite what he'd done and if he should knock again or just go away. Ushering him into the large lounge the distraught lady explained that her daughter had been simply embarrassed at the state of her hair. 'She shouldn't mind me seeing her in her roll-ons,' Robert said graciously trying to help. The good lady gulped and managed to continue the conversation somehow. Later Robert was relating the events of the day to his kind landlady, Mrs Whitten, when she collapsed in laughter.

'You didn't really say that, did you?' she said, wiping the tears from her eyes.

'What's wrong?' Robert asked mystified at her mirth.

'You meant "rollers", not "roll-ons," ' she said, 'I bet you'll not be let into that house again!'

One of the greatest thrills Robert had was that of leading a couple to commit their union to Jesus. They had lived together unmarried for many years. To be present at their marriage where all the children paraded into church was indeed an occasion of celebration. In retrospect Robert said it made that whole year worth while.

Robert grew to love Fermanagh in that short year and a bit. It was such a completely different environment from Hunter Street. The wide open spaces with fields and rolling hedgerows as far as the eye could see in sharp contrast to row upon row of square edged terrace houses that had been his home for so long, with their harsh man-made, brightly painted brickwork, black tarmacadam roads and flat grey footpaths. Fermanagh was God's natural handiwork, soft mossy grass underfoot ever-changing skies with frolicking clouds. The trees fresh laden with leaves in summer and so bare and stark bending in the winter winds and glistening in the frost. What a mighty God had made all this !

Finishing his term there in June, Robert was preparing to return to Belfast to get organised for his three years in College when he was asked if he would help out in Lisnaskea, a

nearby town, until October when College opened. He readily agreed and his time there was greatly enhanced by the
friendship of an elderly lady, Miss Eva Bell. She was a ready
listener to all the 'Juniors' and was always ready to advise,
taking them all under her wing. A very dear Christian lady
who treated them all as her children.

October came quickly and finally he was driving down
Lennoxvale. He turned into the gates of Edgehill Theological College. Set facing south in its own grounds, it was an
impressive square Victorian-style mansion, with a beautiful
pillared entrance. Once inside the planners seemed to have
lost interest for internally it was an uninteresting structure.
The dull entrance corridor led through to a wide hall with a
stairway that could hardly be called sweeping. The decor
was all very plain and basic, reminiscent of many other
institutions. The theologs' small rooms had basic furniture
of bed, wardrobe and dressing table. The principal's study
downstairs was a dark room lined with books. Rev Richard
Greenwood's large desk sat slightly off-centre where he had
an instant view of callers. The large dining-room was furnished with one long table and some impressive portraits of
previous principals. Upstairs the sitting-room was equipped
with an ancient record-player and a selection of worn
records left by successive students. A couple or rows of
books on a bookcase, a rather tatty array of furniture which
was only held together by its original good workmanship, all
sat on a square of worn carpet, arranged to face the large
open fire-place where a happy coal fire burnt.

This was a dream come true. It seemed a very long time
ago when he had sat in the electric presence of God and
turned his eyes this direction.

To outlay expenses on the college a certain number of
rooms were let out to lay-students needing digs. They usually were from Methodist homes and Christian upbringing
and were studying at Queen's University or somewhere
nearby. They were allocated rooms at one side of the house.
Miss Thomas, the Matron, was a buxom white-haired lady;
or perhaps she only went white after Robert's three college
years. She oversaw the cooking, cleaning and general running of the household. The students long ago had nick-
named her 'Mince Thomas' through her clever ability to
produce the said food in 57 varieties! These boys who could

be so angelic and sing like cherubs at early morning prayers also frequently turned her head with their antics.

The week's curriculum for the students was divided between Edgehill and Assembly's College, the Presbyterian Theological College situated behind Queen's University. The two colleges combined for many parts of the students' training programme.

Walking down Malone Road to Assembly's College on frequent occasions Robert passed nuns journeying to and fro from Aquinas Hall. One in particular was rather pretty and Robert struck up a nodding acquaintance with her. At first Robert was very straight-faced, but as the months passed it became a smile and a wave. The nun would respond with a gentle blushing smile then go her way. This appealed to Robert's mischievous sense of humour. After months of this impish behaviour she caught him out one day when she appeared unexpectedly and spied him in his clerical collar. He waved and grinned. On realising he was the opposition she went very pink and hurried away and ever after refused to look his direction despite all his whistles and waves.

Years on a diet of fish, chips and white bread, washed down by gallons of tea, finally took its toll on Robert. He doubled up one day while walking past the City Hall, and collapsed with the pain. The doctors diagnosed an ulcer and there began a very rough period for Robert's health. Every spare moment he rested and tried to stick to the bland tasteless food prescribed for his complaint. Nothing seemed to improve his condition until someone recommended John Hamilton, a naturopath. Robert decided anything was worth a try. A very rigid regime of salad, fresh fruit, and small amounts of a milky preparation called 'Kummus' were advised along with lots of rest. Robert's stern willpower came into its own as he stuck rigidly to this new way of life. All his lovely habits of multiple cups of tea, large packages of fish and chips had to go and a new attitude to eating began. By June 1966 when we started seeing each other he stuck strictly to cheese salads in restaurants whenever we ate out. Gradually over the next year as he began to feel fitter, he chanced the odd steak with his salad.

At this time Robert's liberal thinking began to be shaken in college, not because of evangelical teaching but the very opposite. As he went through the very liberal thinking behind his training he began to question it and became more and more convinced that fundamental evangelical theology had a lot more basis in Scripture.

The Mods and Rockers of the sixties were in the habit of congregating around the Belfast City Hall. Donegall Square Methodist Church which is situated right beside the City Hall had a large basement hall which they opened as a coffee bar. Edgehill students used to come and counsel these teenagers. Robert took me with him on a few occasions. There was snooker and table tennis, coffee tables and chairs where discussions could be developed. We talked of Jesus Christ and how belonging to him lifted the boredom and gave aim and purpose to life. Discussions developed on evolution and whether the Bible was the infallible word of God, could it all have really begun with just two people, Adam and Eve?; I listened to Robert explain how he thought Adam could mean many men and I began to realise, as he did, how unconvincing the arguments were. My own belief in evolution at that time conflicted with the Bible after a while Robert stopped going. The realisation that he had to get his own thinking sorted out before he could counsel and advise others, became very clear to him. The Biblical truths were beginning to shine through the shallow man-made theories with a crystal clear light that could not be put out.

The College summer holidays were a time to top up funds for the year ahead, so Robert had taken on a job for the 'twelfth' fortnight in July the annual holiday time, as an extra night-watchman in Ewart's Spinning Mill. The factory had been broken into several times and the management thought it wise to employ extra guards over the holidays. So Robert and three others took it in turn to walk the full round of the factory each hour. The walk took a good half-hour. The linen looms were only rested once a year and the quiet night air was punctuated with the cracks and groans of machinery contracting as it cooled. There were stations at various points around the factory that the night-watchmen checked into to ensure the whole factory was covered each time. As the week progressed Robert became more and more tired. Many days he got no sleep at all as he was helping out on the Newtownards circuit and had the congregation to visit during the day and sermons to prepare.

45

The long nights were put in with telling jokes and ghost stories. On the very last night of the fortnight Robert drew the last walk. By now totally exhausted he was very relieved the fortnight was almost over. He walked quickly as he neared the end. He could visualise his warm bed, his soft feather pillow with his head sinking into it as he pulled the covers over his shoulder. He just had to walk down the iron stairs into the boiler-house and he was home and dry. He opened the door and started down when he came to an abrupt halt. There in the middle of the floor lay a body. Feeling it would be unwise to tackle this situation on his own he ran to get the others. They roared with laughter at his distraught state.

'That's the boiler-man' they cackled. 'He's in to light up the boiler. Then he lies flat on the warm floor and has a kip.' Work began again that morning. It was a while before Robert was as amused as they were; he had been thoroughly shaken by the whole affair.

Back to the grindstone Robert was voted in as Chairman of the Students Union in his second year in College. That meant he had responsibility for organising the various preaching appointments, amongst other duties. It also meant taking the more inaccesible services himself. Consequently he travelled to many of the farthest corners of Ulster and on Sundays and when off-duty allowed, I travelled with him. Being Chairman meant keeping a certain amount of peace within the student body. But there were times when mischief overruled responsibility. One of the mature students (they only had to live in for a week), had missed out on the cold baths and Robert and his friend decided to initiate the man. They dismantled his bed and removed it, took out the light bulb, closed the door and with a piece of string flicked the small bolt home so that the door was locked from the inside. In the darkness of Robert's room they waited, endlessly it seemed. There was the sound of heavy feet on the linoleum corridor and the rattling of a door handle. Then a more insistent shaking of the stubborn door, then the sound of a solid shoulder being welted against the door and the sound of feet walking away down the stairs. The friends contained their laughter until silence reigned, then exploded. Wondering what would happen next they were soon put out of their misery as they heard Miss Thomas remonstrating with the gentleman.

Miss Thomas remonstrating with the gentleman.

'What do you need that axe for?'

'Just to break down my door.'

Miss Thomas gasped, 'You can't do that!'

'Just watch me!' he exclaimed and marched forcefully down the steps and round the corner. He took the blunt end to the door and the bolt gave way. Assuring the terrified housekeeper that he would pay for the damage he flicked the light switch to no effect and threw the axe where the bed should have been. It hit the floor with a resounding thud and he turned on his heel and marching back down the corridor he threw over his shoulder, 'I'm going home to my wife!' Miss Thomas went straight to Robert's door and knocked and tried the handle. Finding it locked and getting no answer she went on her way. When all was quiet the boys replaced the light bulb and reassembled the bed.

Robert was called to the principal's study next morning. Standing outside the door he decided it was best to come clean and own up. He would probably be disciplined and lose his prided Chairman's position but the whole episode had been his idea. Standing 'on the mat' Mr Greenwood asked,

'Who is responsible for this outrage?'

Robert opened his mouth to replay. Just at that moment the door opened and Miss Thomas came in.

'There's no use you questioning Mr Bradford,' she said. Robert's mouth fell open in amazement. He shut it again thinking he probably resembled a goldfish.

'He was fast asleep in his room through the whole affair, I tried his door. You know how ill he's been!'

Mr Greenwood turned to Robert. 'I want to know who's responsible for this, that bolt will have to be paid for'.

'Yes, Sir', said Robert, turning on his heel and leaving, not quite believing his good fortune.

At times I remonstrated with Robert about what I felt was his irresponsibility.

'We are steeped in religiosity all day at lectures, then spend our week-ends taking services. We live very close to God,' he said, 'but if we don't let our hair down sometimes we would all go slowly mad.'

Edgehill College was loosely affiliated with Queen's University. This gave the students the opportunity to use the sports facilities. It also meant that Robert could play football for the Queen's Soccer team. Having lost a lot of weight because of his illness he then set about working himself up to full fitness again. An inter-University game was to be played on Stranmillis College playing fields at Shaw's Bridge. A brisk wind was blowing that crisp winter's day and there were some skiffs of rain as the spectators huddled together for warmth. The fairly fast game was well under way on the soft ground when Robert performed a spectacular overhead scissor kick which resulted in a goal. Brought up on rugby, soccer was all new to me. I have never seen anything quite like it before meeting Robert. I was awestruck. A little further on in the game he tried again but it didn't come off.

'Should have known it couldn't have come off twice, Bradford', mumbled his coach beside me, warming himself by slapping his arms around his body. Excitement was hard to work up as my body became so cold that I didn't think my legs or hands belonged to me. The game was over. Queen's had won. I found myself swung off the ground and hugged by an extremely muddy, half blind person who badly needed a shower.

As Chairman, Robert tired of accounting for everyone's movements and finally locking up at night. So he came up with what he felt was the perfect solution to the problem. He got two dozen copies made of the front door key and distributed them to all the students. A better idea than late-comers climbing in by the dining-room window as was the usual case, Robert thought. Invariably they would shake the table where the delft was piled and make a fearful racket, which would in turn wake the Greenwoods' rather noisy poodle.

As part of their training the local prisons were honoured with a delegation of students. Robert and the others, bedecked in their clerical outfits were shown around. It was all fairly light-hearted until Robert came face to face with an old friend. John and Robert had been mates as teenagers when Robert was deciding whether to let Christ take full control of his life or continue in his self-indulgent ways. The scales had tipped the other way for John and he was there paying the price for the way of life he had chosen.

'There but for the grace of God go I,' Robert realised.

The magnitude of what his Lord had delivered him from shook him and he uttered a heartfelt prayer of gratitude to the Almighty.

Another College year over, Robert was off to Cork for a few months. There followed a searching period in his life. He took with him Sangster's book *Pure in Heart*, an essay on sanctification. *'An essay which has cut through the repelling conceit of a self-sufficient young man'* he wrote. How little he had to offer his Lord and yet God had called him and was using him in his great plan.

> *'As I walked tonight in the cold evening air a voice seemed to continually say to me, "What are you?" As I tried to answer I began "I am someone who enjoys his work." Yet the voice seemed to say, "That isn't what I asked you; you may know where you are going and enjoy your work, but – what are you?" Then the whole experience made sense, my love. Over the past few weeks I have been made to face life as it is, not as I would like it to be, made to face myself as I am, not as I would like to think of myself – in short, I have been having an overdue dose of humility. You see, love, at the end of the day I am nothing more than a small part of God's universal vehicle of grace, with no promise of greatness, outstanding success, or even success at all. I can almost sense your reaction, here he goes trying to put me off again! Not this time, love, indeed the very opposite – while I realise I am simply what I am, whatever the future might hold it will have to contend with not merely Robert Bradford, but him and also one on whom he relies greatly, namely my darling Norah. You not only complement the work which I do – your love for me and our mutual love for Christ is the very source of all that I try to do.'*

The farming folk with whom Robert stayed while on the Cork circuit shared his sense of humour. While travelling into Cork city from the farm Robert heard a rumbling and a thud every time he turned a corner. He took the journey more slowly and drove into the first garage he saw.

'I'm afraid it may be something serious, there's a fearful noise.' The car was put up on the hydraulic jack and inspected underneath, then the engine was checked out.

'Anything in the boot, Sir?' asked the mechanic in despair. 'No, nothing,'

Robert replied, 'nothing.' 'Let's try a short trip and maybe I could identify the noise,' suggested the mechanic. Off they went and sure enough at the first sharp corner there was a rumbling and an ominous thud. Back at the garage the mechanic again asked if Robert was sure about the contents of the boot.

'Nothing but the spare wheel, I'll show you,' and he opened the boot. There lay a very large boulder.

'Tom!' said a shocked Robert, in sudden realisation that it had been put there by the son-in-law of the family, in fun. Judging by the look of pity on the mechanic's face, he was clearly thinking, 'Poor lad, must have forgotten his tablets to-day, imagine him talking to a stone!'

Robert removed the boulder and went his way planning his revenge on Tom for his prank.

North again he tackled a different job in Dobson's Dairies. It was an added financial bonus he wasn't expecting. His friend, Jim Rea, had been offered the job and then couldn't take it so Robert stood in, knowing he would need the money before the college year was out. Ice-cream by the gallon seemed the perfect way to spend a few hot summer weeks not realising how sick of the sight of it he would become. How relieved he was when the time was up and the job finished.

Every spare moment that summer we spent together. The 'Sound of Music' had come to a Belfast cinema and Robert had got tickets. One beautiful very hot sunny day we parked the car in a narrow street off Howard Street near the city centre leaving my handbag under the seat and Robert's coat on the back seat covering a brightly wrapped box containing a wedding present. The film was spectacular and we did enjoy it, except for trying to mop choc-ice off my white dress in the dark. We walked happily back to the car only to discover it had been broken into. The side vent had been forced and the contents of my handbag and Robert's coat pocket strewn over the floor. Robert's Parker pen was still there and all his other things, the tea-set was still intact in its box and the only thing missing seemed to be the money out of my purse.

'How much had you?' Robert asked anxiously.

'One and ninepence,' I repled. 'Oh, that's not so bad,' he breathed a sigh of relief.

I wasn't so relieved. That was all I had until next pocket-money day but I sure wasn't going to tell him that. We were both relieved that the car itself was still there, as it could have gone. We drove to Barnetts Park and unloaded the picnic from the boot. We walked down the long grassy slope of the park and found a quiet corner near the trees to spread our rug.

'These sandwiches are chicken, those are salad, and those are banana,' I pointed out and set about pouring coffee.

'Fungus sandwiches, I love fungus sandwiches' Robert said.

'What do you mean?' I said indignantly.

'A girl I took out a long time ago used to feed me those when they were black, but I'm sure your's will be beautiful,' he added hastily as one whizzed past his ear.

The lovely long summer evenings with picnics on the beach, evenings out to the cinema to see some epic, all made the bright days fly by. Robert would call at 'Tara', our lovely sea-side home set on a hill, stay for a meal and a chat with my Dad and Mum. Our spacious lounge was much used in the summer months, with its beautiful sea view of Scotland on clear days through enormous plate glass windows. Dad would lounge in his favourite well-worn chair, Robert would make himself comfortable and together they would put the world to rights, rarely agreeing though, on how it should be done. I steered clear of these discussions because I invariably ended up getting cross with one or other, or both. Tea ready, we would adjourn to the dining-room for salad, home-made wheaten bread, jam and cakes prepared by my hardworking Mum. The evening was then ours as we reversed out of the driveway on to the deeply pot-holed lane and drove away. Driving slowly, one hand on the wheel, one hand clasping mine, we set off down the coast to one of our favourite beaches. Robert crooned 'Catch a falling star, and put it in your pocket, never let if fade away' in a near perfect imitation of Perry Como. The world was our oyster. I had many years training ahead and so had Robert so we felt we had all the time in the world. Those blissfully happy days became cherished memories to us.

Robert's last year in college passed quickly and quite as quickly we were pouring over the first draft of stations then the second a month later and finally we knew definitely. It

51

was Cregagh Methodist Church for the next year at least. This was great news as he could have been sent to anywhere in Ireland. Cregagh was situated on one of the main roads out of Belfast and not more than five miles from the hospital where I was doing my nursing training. Almost Robert's first assignment in Cregagh was to go to camp with the Boys Brigade to Sligo.

> 'The boys and Officers are very friendly,' Robert wrote, 'the food is quite good, except no lettuce. I do miss you very much, though it will only be three days till we meet again. This sounds selfish, I know, but I hope you are missing me as much as I am you. If these days are a guide to the kind of things which will happen in Cregagh we are going to have a great time. All my love and prayers,
>
> > Yours lovingly,
> > Robert.'

Robert threw himself into the work at Cregagh with real fervour. The superintendent minister gave Robert his list for visiting the congregation and he set about finding his way around the various streets and estates and getting to know the individual families, encouraging non-churchgoers to venture out on Sundays. First he got to know them as friends, then appealed to them to honour him with their presence on his territory.

Football had its bad times as well as its successes with the young church team. A nasty sliced knee resulted from a sliding tackle on the Ormeau Park pitch during one of these games. Transported to hospital Robert had it duly cleaned, stitched and bandaged and was about to leave when he was told he had to have an anti-tetanus injection.

'You're not doing it,' he told the nurse, Hardly his usual polite self.

'You're not leaving without it!' she said indignantly.

'Haven't you got a male nurse somewhere around?' Robert asked hopefully. A male nurse eventually came and Robert had his injection.

'You silly idiot,' I told him later when he phoned to say he couldn't drive to collect me as planned.

'The nurse would have been far more gentle with the injection.'

'I wasn't taking my trousers down in front of any female!' he said still smarting from the memory. The next few weeks proved very difficult for Robert as he just couldn't drive. He got very fed up and bored having to wait around for people to deliver him to places. I drove him in my off-duty hours but his visits to the congregation were sadly curtailed. A lesson in patience was being learnt very impatiently.

Robert in his own way was training me as he felt we would soon be a team. 'I want you to see this situation and tell me what you make of it,' he said as he collected me one day after duty. Robert cooked my tea, left the dirty dishes for 'Sadie' as usual despite my objections and we went off in the car. The cold dark winter's night made me shiver. Past Ormeau Park on to the Ravenhill Road we travelled. Robert parked the car down a side street and knocked on a dingy door set in a blank wall. A very grubby, unshaven young man answered our knock and we followed him up the bare wooden stairway to the light shining from the room above. We were in a room about twelve foot square, very stale smelling, furnished with a large dishevelled bed at one side and a very tatty curtain tacked across the window. The floor was bare boards apart from one stained piece of carpet. Large lumps of thick cut crusty bread were strewn across the floor under the square table in the other corner, obviously thrown there by the toddler lying in the middle of the bed, a comforter in his mouth. The child's face was filthy and its nappy had obviously not been changed for a long while. The woman made no effort to bring us into the room. She remained sitting on the bed paying little attention to us. 'Embarrassed' I surmised, but not by her state of cleanliness or the state of the room; I couldn't quite put my finger on it. The man, in his early thirties, was doing all the talking. He stood in front of the door which wouldn't go quite back against the wall. Then I saw the reason why this silver-tongued man was trying to keep us half out of the room. Through the crack in the door I saw the back of a very large colour television set. This man who hadn't money for food or clothes, who was pleading for assistance from Robert from the 'Poor Fund' was not as desperate as he was letting on. We left without making any promises.

'What did you make of that, love?' Robert said when we were safely in the car.

'He's not as genuine as he lets on,' I said, 'did you see that TV behind the door?'

'He came to the church this morning with a real sob story and I fell for it. He said he hadn't eaten in four days so I took him home and opened a large tin of baked beans, cooked half a pound of sausages and made some Smash and put it all in front of him with a pot tea and he only picked at it. I still wasn't sure. Maybe if he hadn't eaten for days he genuinely couldn't eat so I took him to the Grosvenor Hall. He was very reluctant to go but he was in my car and had no choice. He was instantly recognised as a lazy con-man who had been around every charity in the city.' Robert still didn't like to write him off completely. If the chap was living on his wits trying to con money off churches and charities, he had to at least be given 'ten for trying.' The child was obviously going to suffer if something wasn't done about the situation. What a way for a little one to start its life. Robert, always conscious of his own beginnings, got the social services involved with the family and they were given some food vouchers for the sake of the toddler.

'I want you to be able to pick out the con-men from the genuinely needy. It's not easy but we'll meet plenty of both sorts before we're on this road much longer.'

By June of 1969 when my dear Dad passed on, the political situation in our little province was hotting up. Agnes Street Methodist Church situated half way up the Shankill Road was in the centre of a very troubled area. Re-enforcements were appealed for to help curb the gang warfare that was at that time overtaking the streets. In the evening abuse-throwing would escalate to stones and knives. Several of the young ministers would be on hand. Robert tried to work up a rapport with these boys for most were teenagers. He memorised many names as this had a much greater effect in an emergency situation. He watched their antics and spotted the ringleaders. They often stayed out of sight egging their mates on from cover. Petrol bombs and bullets then began to enter the scene and life on the front line as peacemaker became highly dangerous. Many an evening I feared for his safety, quite expecting to be called to Casualty to tend his wounds along with all the other casualties that poured in from all areas. Sadie and Jimmy Nicholson had moved out of town to a rather nice suburban housing executive estate some years earlier, but Aunt Liz still lived in Hunter Street. Tension was very high in that staunch Protestant area that bordered on an equally staunch Republican area, so Robert set about trying to get her a pensioner's dwelling out of town. But the Lord had it all arranged. A flat became vacant in a small old peoples' section of the same estate not two minutes walk from the Nicholson's door and with the aid of a lorry Aunt Liz was moved in rapidly for fear of squatters. Perhaps the heightening tension and the loss I had sustained forged links between us that had grown loose but our rather battered relationship began to mend. I went to Dartford near London for a holiday and met this rather nice boy, but somehow he didn't really match up.

'Since you've been away,' Robert wrote, 'I have been able to feel something of what it would be like without you, and it was the most depressing feeling I've ever had. My darling, God will bring us together, I know, but please be patient with me and above all forgive me for much of the heartbreak which I've caused you over the past months.'

'There is definitely hope for us,' I thought, 'I think I should go away more often.'

From then to December we traversed many hills and valleys in our relationship but with a definite underlying feeling that we were having more hills than valleys. We decided the time had come to get engaged. I was in study block that December week and had the Saturday off. We arranged with Robert's brother-in-law in Armagh to call on him. He was a jeweller. Getting into the car we were both very excited. Then I spied his football kit.

'You can't mean you're going to play today!' I exclaimed.

'I couldn't get out of it,' he explained. 'With wanting to keep our engagement a secret till Christmas Day I couldn't say why I wasn't free. I will play while you go and show your ring to your mum and then you pick me up and we'll tell my folks.'

That winning smile always softened me up. I was determined nothing would spoil that day, so I put football firmly out of my mind.

It was pouring as we parked on the street nearby and ran into the shop. Billy, Robert's brother-in-law was down the back mending jewellery. Swinging up the steps on his crutches he greeted us warmly. Robert and he asked after respective family members.

'Hide all the large expensive rings please Billy,' Robert teased.

'Mind you, she looks like she'd be worth spending a bob or two on,' Billy suggested, eyeing me with a grin.

The teasing went on incessantly and I sat down patiently to wait until they had both finished. Finally the trays of rings that were within Robert's price range were brought out and we set to to choose one. What seemed a very long time later I had decided on a two-stone diamond twist. Robert approved and then promptly feigned a faint when he saw the price. He then chose a signet ring to suit his well-groomed square hands. Rather nice hands I thought.

'I can engrave your initials on it now if you like? Bill suggested. It took us both to persuade Robert to put all three initials as he really had an aversion for his middle name 'Jonathan'. Finally he agreed that three would look better than two and Billy set to work. Travelling back towards Belfast we were both very content. Robert looked happier than I'd seen him for some time.

'We're not making a mistake,' I ventured as I turned his shiny new gold signet ring on his finger.

'No, I know we're not,' he said smiling happily. 'Do you really like it?' he added.

'The ring's really super. I'm glad we didn't have to alter the size.' I said.

We said goodbye at Newtownards both with our gloves on to hide our shiny rings.

My brother Dermot was working at his car when I arrived, and he gave me an enormous hug. I explained Robert's absence and went to find Mum.

A couple of hours later I was heading back to Newtownards, gloves on again because I wanted the official announcement to be when all the family were together later that week for Christmas Day. It was much simpler than travelling the length and breadth of Ulster to tell them all.

I was supposed to be off on holiday after study block but a shortage on the new ward I was to go to meant I had been asked to go on night-duty that evening for the whole week.

On Sunday I got up mid-afternoon and Robert picked me up at Bostock House Nurses' Home on the Falls Road.

'I have a confession,' Robert said when he had kissed me. 'I'm afraid it's out in Cregagh.' He looked rather sheepish. 'I forgot to take my ring off for church and a few people noticed it.'

'Forgot?' I said disbelieving, yet secretly pleased that it was too much for him to keep quite about.

'Well sort of,' he added.

'My family don't even know yet,' I said. The importance of that to me was lost on him.

'Maybe no-one'll spread it before Christmas Day,' he ventured.

'Methodists are like a bush telegraph system,' I protested, 'It's probably known in Fermanagh and Cork by now. And I've got to walk into church tonight in Cregagh.'

Congratulations poured in, then presents began arriving. When the third clock was presented to us from various organisations in Cregagh, Robert commented, 'Do you think they might be hinting at my time-keeping?'

We set the wedding date for December 5th, 1970 – almost a year away, and arrangements got under way. The new Chapel of Unity at Methodist College, Belfast, was our choice of venue for the service as the size was ideal, plenty of parking space and it was in Belfast, easier for a lot of people to get to than Donaghadee. The memorial stained glass window dedicated to my father's memory was as close as I could get to having my dad there at the ceremony. A nearby hotel was booked for the reception, and the photographer arranged.

The stationing draft announced that Suffolk was where Robert was to spend his first years after ordination in June. A church extension charge and a real opportunity to work for our Lord. A new church building was about to be started and Robert thought he had been handed a parcel from heaven. The manse was not large, isolated, dark or draughty but a bright modernised semi-detached house in a pleasant avenue about a mile and a half from Suffolk church. July came and he had to say his goodbyes to Cregagh and I realised how many real friends we had made amongst the congregation. The final quarterly meeting of

57

the leaders on the circuit was to take place in Glenburn Church. 'You're invited,' Robert chuckled at my expression.

'What for?' I asked, knowing fine but not wanting to believe it.

'A presentation, And don't take longer than twenty minutes to reply, please, love as there's a lot of business to get through,' he teased.

My worst fears realised, I gulped.

'You can reply as the official head of this combination. How many people will be there?' I queried warily.

'Not more than two hundred, the hall only seats that.' The thought of facing ten people without saying anything filled me with dread, knowing Robert's powers of exaggeration, I reckoned on there being probably fifty people at the most. When I walked into the crowded hall I wished I had believed him. There really were about two hundred people chatting away gaily to each other. The happy chorus of chatter was hushed and the meeting began. A hymn was sung and they went to prayer. The gentle reverent silence was disturbed when an elderly gentleman entered the door rather noisily. Already very nervous I didn't like to look up and hastily shut my eyes again and tried to regain my concentration. It was not to be. He had sat down in my row. The two ladies who had joined me were dunted in the ribs, 'Want a sweet?' the gentleman whispered loudly, pushing a bag under their noses. As their shoulders began to shake I looked up and he caught my eye. The bag was pushed noisily toward me and I tried vainly to ignore him. Finally the prayer ended and the gentleman sat back now prepared to be a little quieter. The business of the evening dealt with, a large brightly wrapped parcel was lifted out from behind the piano and Mrs McClintock, a very dear friend, presented me with the gift of a lovely green coffee set. Then it was time for me to reply. I managed all of two sentences from a very red face and sat down glowing profusely and allowed Robert to continue the speech of thanks.

The Grosvenor Hall was packed for the ordination service. 'Let love come first' was Robert's theme for his part of the moving ceremony. He took time to thank the Nicholsons for all they had done for him and to dedicate what he hoped God had in store for our future together.

Suffolk's small Methodist congregation met in the local community centre which also served as bingo hall during the week. The white low-set church hall that they had been using until recently was the site for the new building and was due to be demolished. This tumble-down building which had housed services for many years held a special place in the hearts of many of the congregation. Its broken floors held memories of many happy days, its now empty fireplace had glowed with radiant heat most days of the weeks of the years gone by. The mice now had free run above and below the broken floorboards.

Once I had recovered sufficiently from my appendicectomy to attend services it was easy for me when off duty to come up, attempt cleaning the house and attend some meetings.

Robert gathered a nucleus of people around him and infused them with his enthusiasm. He re-organised the filing and arranged things to be easy at hand for himself. Then he looked at the way visitations had been carried out and reorganised that into streets and areas and classes, taking a leaf out of Cregagh's book. Anything further to that he took the wise advice he had been given by an elderly clergyman friend, 'Don't change anything in a church until you have been in it a year and can judge how it works.' It proved to be good advice. When time is spent discussing changes over a long time then gradually eased into it doesn't hurt so many feelings. Even better if you had the gift Robert had of suggestion. I watched him work in amazement. He would think of an idea and put the seeds of it into a discussion. The people involved would then separately all come up with his original idea. They would get together and say

'Would this not be the best way to tackle this problem?'

'I don't know,' he would often reply, 'have you thought it through, will it work?'

Since it was their own they worked much harder at it and were not offended at him all the time making the suggestions. The Suffolk people were so very friendly and accepted me so readily that I found my shyness fading.

With the manse being fully furnished we didn't need much by way of expensive items of furniture. Two rocking chairs, a fridge and a television were the only large extras needed. The church leaders' board informed us that if we

59

went to Hoggs, a local china shop, a certain amount of money was available for us to purchase a dinner set of china. Absolutely thrilled, I set off one day with my Mum to choose from the glittering galaxy of tableware on show. How would I decide? Then out of the corner of my eye I spied 'Pastorale', a Royal Doulton design I had seen years before in a friend's house and had loved from that day. I ventured a look at the price and discovered to my amazement it was cheaper than others I had looked at and not liked as much. The decision was made and I went back to Upper Green to tell Robert the glad news.

A congregational social evening had been prepared for the presentation. The Walsh Hall, a small wooden hall on stilts was gaily decorated for the occasion. There on display on a table at the top and was not only the dinner set but a matching tea-set, an electric kettle and an electric blanket.

A whole evening of music was provided by the choir and some visiting soloists. I was very impressed. This small closely knit community were willing and anxious to welcome us both. After supper Robert thanked everyone for their generous gifts and commented, 'I don't know what's the point in giving me an electric blanket now when I could have used if for the last five months and I'll not need it from now on.'

I held my breath but they took it well and the rest of the evening relaxed into an easy time of getting to know these people I was soon to be working amongst. The evening over, we were leaving, I had to get back to Donaghadee that night. As we walked out we were suddenly showered with confetti and rice. It was in my hair, in my ears, over and in my clothes and a long battle ensued, enjoyed by everyone. Finally we escaped.

'They're really nice people', Robert said brushing rice out of my hair as he drove. 'We're going to enjoy our time here.' Robert took my hand, intertwined our fingers and gave me one of his winning smiles.

The big wedding day was finally here. Robert was leaving for the church from Upper Green. The best-man, Jim Rea, arrived in plenty of time for them to organise themselves. Robert had purchased a large book for his friend, for undertaking the task of getting him hitched Jim sat down with a large mug of coffee and a few sustaining chocolate biscuits to peruse the volume on his knee. A lengthy discussion followed and it would still have been in progress hours later but for the timely intervention of our kind next-door neighbour Kathleen Good.

'Aren't either of you going anywhere this morning?' she suggested. The two hastily got dressed and managed to make it to the church before I did. Black narrow-legged suits, clerical collars and red carnations in their button holes. Shoes highly polished, Jim's hair greased flat and Robert's waves carefully moulded into place, each hair obeying its master's firm combing. Standing at the altar knowing I had arrived Robert's heart began beating loudly in his ears.

The ceremony and service seemed to be over very quickly and we were in the vestry signing the register and walking back down through the church. 'How do I lead you out?' he asked nervously. Outside the church the cameras clicked incessantly and the confetti flew around. Wtih Robert grasping my hand firmly I was the happiest person in the world at that moment. 'Married,' I thought. How often since that day back in June, 1967, when he proposed, had I wondered if this day would ever really be. We were into the limousine and off to the blazing log fire awaiting us at the hotel reception. The dry brisk winter's day held for the photographs with only a very little drizzle as we finished. The meal was delicious and the people I had seated together seemed to be getting on well. Upstairs changing, Barbara, my bridesmaid, and I watched with delight as my brothers scoured the surrounding area in search of our get-away car. As we were being driven off by Ken in his car they would have a long search. Ken proceeded to take our cases out. Not knowing my family very well he didn't fight too hard and our cases were captured. 'Oh well' I sighed, 'I hope the extra rice and confetti won't make our baggage overweight.'

Running the gauntlet to get to the car was delightfully difficult. Finally we escaped.

3

Staying overnight in London had been a good idea as it enabled us to empty out all the confetti and rice and start off afresh with some hope of pretending we weren't on honeymoon. We boarded the Dan Air flight to Tunis, the capital of Tunisia. Neither of us had travelled far by plane and so it was very exciting; the scary thrill as that enormous plane thrust forward at high speed along the runway pushing us back into our seats. The humidity hit us as we disembarked and we sweltered in our heavy clothes in the coach to the Hotel. What an impressive white arch entrance gate! The low spread-eagled Hotel main building had cool marble floors with refreshing air-conditioned lounges.

The days passed quickly as we walked in and out to the quaint walled village of Hammammet which held the local shops. The sharp contrast between the luxury mansions situated in the orange groves, the local people, then on down the scale to the fly-covered beggars was rather frightening. The taxi drivers ruled the road, they put their hand hard on the horn and drove down the centre of the road and if you didn't get out of the way, too bad!

Bargaining for souvenirs was immense fun; the shopkeepers plied us with little cups of thick black bitter coffee, pretending to be so hurt by our offers, bargaining until we both reached a compromise was so much more fun than normal shopping. All to soon it was time to go home.

At the door of No. 35 Upper Green I waited until Robert unlocked the door then stood there.

'You can't mean it,' he said.

'Yes I do.'

He put down the cases he was carrying and made a real meal of lifting me over the threshold, panting and staggering into the hall.

February 1971 we had the stone-laying ceremony at Suffolk for our new dual purpose building. It looked so small to us walking through the mud, stepping over the door thresholds from room to room as the brick walls rose skywards day by day. It was very exciting watching it grow. The ceremony took place in the rain in the square block which was to be the entrance hall. The hymn epitomised our feelings just then with hope in our hearts and faith in our Saviour.

'Jesus where'er Thy people meet
There they behold Thy mercy seat;
Where'er they seek Thee Thou art found
And every place is hallowed ground.

Dear Shepherd of Thy chosen few,
Thy former mercies here renew;
Here to our waiting hearts proclaim
The sweetness of Thy saving name.

Here may we prove the power of prayer
To strengthen faith and sweeten care,
To teach our faint desires to rise,
And bring all heaven before our eyes.

Lord, we are few, but Thou art near.
Nor short Thine arm nor deaf Thine ear;
O rend the heavens, come quickly down,
And make a thousand hearts Thine own.'

The short service ended with a prayer . . . 'Grant O Lord that as we prepare to build Thee a House, so our hearts may be prepared to worship Thee worthily within it; through Jesus Christ our Lord.'

Robert decided to join the Orange Preceptory and so became part of Cross of St. Patrick LOL 688 (Loyal Orange Lodge 688). There followed quickly offers to preach at various gatherings. This new-found fame Robert coped with very well. I was rather more awed by the large captive audiences for his preaching than he. At one service he was asked to receive the offering. 'Forgive us for the sixpences, thrupenny bits and pennies. Help us to give You back what you really deserve . . . our lives.' It caused rather a murmuring and the baskets were sent round again to relieve everyone's conscience.

'You chanced your arm' I commented after.

'I meant it,' he said, then he chuckled, 'they sat up and listened afterwards, didn't they. Someone has to shake them out of their apathy.'

Being married to Robert meant life was full of the unexpected. I woke one night in the small hours thinking I was in the middle of an earthquake. The whole bed was shaking. I touched Robert's shoulder to see if he was awake and he errupted with convulsive laughter. When he calmed down slightly he said,

'You'll have to hear this joke I heard to-day.'

I sat waiting in amazement while he related the latest joke which he was finding so hilarious. He turned over still chuckling and went happily back to sleep while I was left to lie awake for hours. It was a situation I often found myself in.

In May we were off to London to take part in a Methodist Association of Youth Clubs weekend. Our young people along with other Methodist teenagers from other circuits were to perform in the Royal Albert Hall. We couldn't afford for me just to come along so I had to help in the pageant. I don't think I've ever felt a bigger fool. The highlight for the week-end was the Sunday Service at which Cliff Richard sang.

The 12th July had arrived and the church members were bustling around from early morning at the 'Field' where the Orange Order Parade was to have its service. 'The Field' was situated on the outskirts of Belfast in Finaghy, fairly close to Andersonstown. Because tension in the province was seriously high the road to Andersonstown, a Roman Catholic area, was roped off at a motorway bridge and police and army guarded the parade in case of attackers. The day went well and some money was made for church funds, by sale of teas and sandwiches to the weary marchers.

At the top of Lenadoon Avenue in Suffolk the Housing Executive Estate had been linked up with the Roman Catholic Andersonstown Estate, consequently there was an easy escape route for trouble makers. Many Roman Catholic and Protestants had lived for many years together without a problem, but where there were troublemakers on the Roman Catholic side, our Tartan gangs of youths would retaliate on the other. If some of our windows in the homes in Suffolk were broken then the same happened in Andersonstown and many peaceful people on both sides found themselves in the middle of a battlefield.

Night after night Robert was called out often taking me

64

with him to comfort some family who were terrified. In August, in one night an estimated two hundred Protestant families fled. They moved their furniture by lorry, by van, even on car roof racks. The Tartan gangs were organised to assist in an effort to keep the houses occupied and therefore cause less retaliation. A meeting was called in the Community Centre and strong resolutions were passed with the tough men vowing to stick it out to the last man. Close to Robert a woman lit up her cigarette, intent on the proceedings she didn't shake the match out properly before replacing it in the box. The whole box exploded, she screamed and threw it in the air. Within seconds the hall had emptied. 'hard' men first, women and children last!

Recounting the incident to me Robert roared with laughter. 'If you'd seen their sheepish faces when they found out what they'd run from.' It worried us though because it showed how terribly afraid the people were for their lives. People in the area turned to Robert at every occasion, he was simply known as 'The Vicar' and I as 'Mrs Vicar.' Time and again we would arrive to quieten a mob incited by some means or another to hear the comment go through the ranks . . . 'It's OK, the Vicar's here.' The confidence shown in him by the people he took very seriously and did everything within his power to calm every situation. He negotiated with the police and army personnel, putting the people's point of view, trying to enlighten new battalions of troops as they changed over. On one occasion an army colonel just wouldn't listen and we had the ludicrous situation of a mob of several hundred descending down the hill on Suffolk to burn Protestants out of their homes and the army being told to guard the mob from the people defending their homes, numbering no more than twenty or thirty, as most men were at work! The police thankfully had the situation more in hand and all ended fairly peacefully. The residents were very annoyed by this kind of behaviour and many times sought to take the law into their own hands. Only the fact that Robert continually involved their leaders in his dialogues with the authorities, so that they could see the progress, kept tempers in check.

With the exodus of sixty Methodist families in one night we began to think we would have the opening and closing ceremony of our new building in one day.

Lenadoon Avenue was emptying from the top down and we soon realised the tactics. A spearhead force of about ten families took over each home that was vacated by a fleeing Protestant and gradually worked their way down the hill. No-one wanted to be the end house as it took the brunt of any attacks and therefore home by home was vacated, generally late at night so that the neighbours they had vowed to support didn't see them leave.

Robert and many of the men of the area tried to hold these houses in a vain attempt to halt the terrorists progress. Each person took an empty house and took turns at occupying it despite the torrential rain and cold. Robert came home simply to wring out his sopping wet duffle coat, have a hot bath, some food and return.

A certain gentleman in the area was a fund of information, but always two days after everyone else knew it. Known to the locals as 'MI5' he spoke out of the corner of his mouth, presumably in case anyone should overhear. 'MI5', Robert and two other men were standing near the top of Lenadoon Avenue one day about noon, the torrential rain had ceased for a short time and the sun had come out. The army post opposite was in an empty house on the corner of Falcarragh Drive and Lenadoon Avenue. While the men chatted together and MI5 divulged his latest information, a lorry sped down the hill, it swung right into Falcarragh and up popped a terrorist in the back with a machine gun riddling the army post with gun-fire. The bullets ricocheted across the road to the men. Robert and the others dived for cover, one man straight through the shattering lounge window, another put his shoulder to the door and Robert found himself in the hall, how he got there he wasn't sure. It was all over just as quickly as it had occurred. MI5 was found lying flat on his back in the quagmire of the sodden garden pleading with the Almighty about the state of his good suit seemingly unconcered at his close brush with death.

Travelling to work at the hospital could be a slow business and often army vehicle check points meant long delays. The quickest way was through the Republican Andersonstown straight down the Falls Road. The army could not set up check points there for fear of snipers using one of the many sympathetic homes around to pick them off, instead the check points were set up on all access roads to the area. As Suffolk and the 'Royal' hospital were both in the one area it was quicker to go straight through. Driving one day I became conscious that the traffic had become so sparse that there was only one other car ahead of me, none behind when I looked in the mirror and none approaching. 'Whoops' I thought, 'there's trouble afoot.' I was just slowing down thinking of turning back as I rounded a bend in the road. The mob, a hundred yards ahead, let out a yell of delight as the lorry they had hijacked caught alight and a great sheet of flames rose towards the clear blue sky. The car in front had done a U-turn and was already approaching me very fast. I swung our heavy dark green Triumph car round and raced after it. The area was deserted, not a soul was in sight along the wide road. I sped homeward, scared to think what I might be heading into as I had a mile to go. I had almost reached a roundabout. Coming up Kennedy Way on the left was another mob. I put my foot to the floor and negotiated the roundabout on two wheels just before the mob got there. I hit the road in spots until I got to Suffolk. Very badly shaken I decided a day off work was in order.

That was the start of a bad few weeks. To the left hand side of the church was a private housing development, mostly Roman Catholic, that we used as a through road to Finaghy from time to time. Barricades were on all terrorist controlled roads for those particular days. Robert drove through the estate and turned down into that private development. Young boys had the road partially blocked, their faces covered with balaclava helmets or scarves. Robert drove straight at them and they jumped out of the way. They shouted and we realised there was a further group fifty yards ahead. I was really frightened then, we were trapped. They quickly blocked the road and the youths reached into the hedge for their concealed weapons. Robert rolled the window down and shouted to the nearest boy as we screached to a halt beside him.

'What do you think you're doing Seamus?'

The youth started, fear registered in his eyes.

'Didn't know it was you Sir,' not wanting to say Robert's name. 'Move the barrier, he's OK.'

We drove on and I sank into the seat weak with relief. Seamus attended our youth club from time to time with some of his friends. How Robert managed to recognise him in his black terrorist garb and scarf, I had no idea. No fear has registered on Robert's face, only anger. Anger that youngsters of twelve, thirteen and fourteen were being taught to be terrorists.

The lighter side to the troubles in Suffolk was sometimes provided by the teenage Tartan gangs. The terrorist supporters at the top of the hill on bright sunny days would bring out their hi-fi- equipment and play Republican songs as loud as they could for our benefit, the Tartan boys would respond by bringing out the pipe band and marching around the streets at the bottom, out of sniper range and playing *The Sash* and other Loyalist songs at full throat.

As time passed the spearhead terrorist group forced its way further down Lenadoon Avenue house by house. The residents were panic stricken again, no-one liked to be the last house, as one family moved so did the next.

At long last it was the night before the grand opening Service. Our new church completed we took a final look around touching the furnishings with joy and tenderness as we went. The sanctuary was a semi-circle on the long wall of the sand coloured brickfaced rectangular building. Capable of being closed off by two enormous concertina doors that folded out of the wall to leave a bare rectangular building with high windows that were unlikely to suffer any damage from games. The circular white side pulpit with black base was backed in the centre by a magnificent stained glass window depicting the cross. At Robert's suggestion the architect had incorporated a few portions of red glass to lighten the effect of the cross, whilst in the centre of the cross was a magnificent twelve-pointed star. The communion rail and table of beech and polished stainless steel sat on a rich blue carpet and gave a very modern effect and toned beautifully with the wooden tongue and groove, varnished, gently sloping ceiling. The stackable black padded chairs were very comfortable. We lined them in rows with aisles of the same rich blue carpet. The effect was astonishingly beautiful for such a simple building. The organ had a special trolley made for it to move it easily into place for services. The choir room which doubled in size with folding doors, the fitted kitchen, the storerooms, the vestry, ladies and gents incorporated the whole suite of premises of which we were all justly proud.

The joyful opening service at which the choir sang like angels was immediately followed by a two week Mission in the church. The theme was *Behold the Lamb of God*. Salvation Army bands had been asked to help and like the Pied Piper, Robert went round the estate asking people to come to the services. The band then made its way to the church and assisted with the hymn singing. The people rallied round and every night people gave their lives to Jesus Christ. But where God is at work Satan tries to get a finger in. Practically every night a squabble would develop in the church before the service and it wasn't until Robert pointed out what was happening and we prayed about it that peace was restored. On the last night of the Mission the title was 'Conversion or Evasion', the Holy Spirit was moving in that little building so fast that the air was electric. *Have you any room for Jesus?* the choir sang quietly and encouragingly.

Robert had been away taking another service, he walked into the church to see the communion rail packed, people were kneeling and standing row upon row. Young people committing their lives for the first time to their Lord, others recommitting lives that hadn't been Christ-centred. The wonder of that sight lived with us a long time and so began the real work in Suffolk. In the weeks and months that followed person after person sought the Lord and committed their lives.

The activities for the winter began with real zest and enthusiasm. Boys Brigade, Girls Brigade, Youth Club, Women's Department, Prayer and Bible Study Group. Every inch of the building was used.

Robert volunteered some of the young women into having a coffee morning once a week. I made the scones and they made the coffee, served it and cleared up after. It became a morning that was really looked forward to by many pensioners who could come and chat with their friends for the whole morning. It was well supported and became a great success bringing in funds towards the debt on the building fund.

Families were still moving out of Suffolk at a fierce rate. Snipers were using the flats at the top of Lenadoon to take pot shots at the Army. In discussion one evening with the Bible Study Group one of the ladies made the suggestion that in the name of Jesus Christ we bind the power of darkness in the area. It seemed such a simple idea we all wondered why we hadn't thought of it before. We went to prayer and in the name of Jesus Christ our Saviour we asked that Satan's hands be tied in Suffolk, that no policeman or soldier would lose their life protecting us. In all our time there not one policeman or soldier was killed even though it was the very heart of the fighting for many years.

Many of our services were conducted with army saracens guarding the doors of the church. Frequently we had army feet running up and down the roof to escape the gunfire being directed at them.

By this time the local residents had banded themselves together in what they called the UDA, the Ulster Defence Association. They armed themselves with axe handles, air rifles and some legally held shot guns. They were no match for the sophisticated weaponry of the IRA terrorists but at least they felt they could defend their homes more adequately.

A few members of the 'Tartan' overheard a woman in the shops complaining how near the spearhead families were getting to her home half way down Lenadoon Avenue.

'There's an empty house in Mizen Gardens, we'll move ya! What number do ya live in?'

Without further ado the lorry was off. They walked in the front door.

'Are you Mr Stevens?'

'Aye.'

They proceeded, without further comment to the man sitting watching the TV, to clear the house of all furniture, carpets and furnishings. At last they got to the lounge where Mr Stevens was still watching TV.

'Is that your chandelier?'

The man nodded and the youth swung on it ripping it out of the ceiling. As he left the room his mate unplugged the TV and lifted it.

'Grab your fags, you're living in Mizen Gardens,' they shouted to the man standing in the middle of the bare room. The lorry took off with his wordly goods and the man walked nonchalantly down the hill towards Mizen Gardens, amazingly unconcerned by the whole affair.

For a lot of the more elderly people, life was as bewildering. The young people in the church banded together and began to do messages for the folk who were too scared to go out of their door. It was a very real problem as the pensioners' bungalows were at the bottom of the grassy hill which flanked Lenadoon and therefore were in line of the sniper fire.

Our church building with its tall internally lit neon stainless steel cross surrounded by brick, shining like a beacon in the area, became a symbol of hope to a lot of people. It also became a spot for target practise for snipers. Some of the church leaders and myself were standing on the freshly laid tarmacadam outside the front of the church one evening at dusk. We were chatting together when there was a crackling in the distance. So used to gunfire I paid little heed, I turned to continue the conversation to find the others all lying flat on their faces . . . 'GET DOWN' they yelled and grabbing my hands pulled me on to my face. The tiny sparks that had been flying were tracer bullets and hadn't missed our heads by very much. When we looked at the church wall later they had hit the brickwork just above where we had been standing.

Since the beginning of the troubles barricades had appeared all over Ulster. Cars were hijacked, often set on fire and the burnt out wreckages used to seal off roads. More often it was buses or lorries. The bus companies and some firms tried to keep a service going to make life as normal as possible but often at a colossal cost. Many small businesses finding themselves in 'no mans land' went bankrupt because they could not get supplies or raw materials in or merchandise out to their clients. At the bottom of Lenadoon one drizzly Sunday the army had a barricade of saracens, completely blocked Lenadoon Avenue and the soldiers lined up facing the hill to ward off the mob of several thousands that was gathering to take over Suffolk. There were very few soldiers in comparison. That drizzly Sunday afternoon the whole of Suffolk waited. The mob moved, led by their leaders, with a lorry full of furniture for use as a battering ram. The saracens pushed them back and they retaliated with snipers. The battle raged and as dusk came and it was time for the service, the women gathered into the church. Their usual cheerful chatter dulled to a frightened whisper.

We gathered round in a semi-circle and after singing a hymn we went to prayer. Robert stole in quietly, strain and anxiety written all over his face. He sat down beside me and just drank in the atmosphere. Realising he wasn't needed, refreshed and calmed by God's presence in that place he quietly went out again to join the army on the front line where he had been. The army won the day and the mob dispersed. Our dejected, frightened people went back to their homes wondering about the tomorrows.

Frequently alone in the manse, I insisted we get a dog, at least that was the excuse. By February '72 I saw the advertisement I had been looking for. 'Yorkshire terrier pups for sale.' I phoned the Ballymoney number and the lady said she had one dog left. She would keep it for me. Robert couldn't come, so my friend, our organist Valerie, volunteered. Off we set on that chilly day going slowly because the roads were quite frosty. I didn't know Ballymoney at all and without directions we would not have found the house. The lady opened the door and ushered us into her sitting-room with a smile.

'He's asleep,' she said.

'But he's not here!' I said in dismay.

She pointed to a cushion on the sofa, a tiny blob of black fur could just be seen under it. I picked up the cushion and the tiny bundle uncurled and stretched itself to its full six inches. I nuzzled him to my face and he licked me. Valerie had to have her turn so I took the opportunity to pay the lady and pedigree papers in hand, we left. Fully awake now he wanted to play and Valerie had a lovely time with him as I drove home. Finally 'Towser' crawled up on my shoulder and settled down for a sleep under the black simulated fur collar of my midi-length coat.

Twinbrook Housing Executive Estate further out of town towards Lisburn was growing in size and several displaced families from Suffolk had been given homes there. The streets were beautifully named after trees, flowers or shrubs. Azalea Gardens, Juniper Walk, etc., and it gave an air of fragrance as you walked along. A set of three huts in the centre of the estate were designated for the use of churches. A Roman Catholic Chapel, a Community Centre and the Protestant denominations shared the third. It worked very well, Protestants and Roman Catholics living together amicably in a fifty-fifty estate, until an influx of about one hundred and thirty Roman Catholic squatters arrived overnight. The residents banded together, Catholic and Protestant, to try to stem the flow but were told they could not block the roads and the influx continued. The small congregation that Robert had carefully nurtured found themselves outnumbered two to one and started looking elsewhere for accommodation once again.

The Sunday night Youth Group which was held in the manse had expanded to about thirty youngsters. The majority headed into the green lounge, battling for the best seats on the brown suite, some into the dining room to capture the green rocking chairs and the main overflow onto the stairs. Some could be found practising guitars in our turquoise bathroom with its frilly net curtains and dark green carpet; that was if you could get as far as the bathroom over the numerous bodies sprawled across the grey carpeted hall and stairs. We had a lot of fun with those young people over coffee and biscuits. Complaints reached my ears one evening.

'Mrs' as they called me, 'have you had any biscuits yet?'

'No,' I replied, I'd been too busy making coffee to have any. A look at the delegation's faces told me something was up. I inquired.

'They're terrible!' They didn't usually mince their words. I tasted one out of the tin, they were definitely awful! I lifted the top layer out and the bottom layer was worse. The paper on the bottom was soaked in petrol. Robert had been carrying a can of petrol in the boot of the car for the lawnmower, some had got spilt and a crack in the biscuit tin must have allowed the petrol to soak up as he transported them home from the shop. We unceremoniously threw them out.

We had been married quite a while now and I felt Robert had adjusted to married life better than I had expected. His fierce independence was still difficult to live with but he was trying to include me in decision-making. I found I could not push him to do something around the house, nagging just didn't work so I tried the 'helpless' routine. I usually drove to work in the car and Robert walked to Suffolk as he liked the exercise. Very few members of the congregation were outside a mile radius of the church so Robert felt it kept him fit. I was usually home first at tea-times. I listened for his arrival as I prepared tea and as he opened the door I would have myself strategically placed in the dining room with a few struck matches on the hearth pretending to light the fire.

'Oh this won't light,' I would sigh exasperatedly as he entered the door.

'I'm sorry your tea's not ready yet,' I added for good measure. I hoped I would be forgiven by the Almighty for my white lies. He fell for it every time and after a few months he automatically lit it and carried in the coal. A gentle reminder occasionally, 'You're so good at it . . . I'm hopeless,' worked a treat. As in any city or community, there were in our area marriages that were going through difficult patches, and children in need. Time and again our spare room was needed by a family in distress. A mother had to go into hospital and her little girl was going to have to go to relatives on the other side of town where it would not be easy for her father to see her. Robert came in one evening and discussed the situation with me. What could be done? I jumped in with both feet.

'She can stay here with us.'

Robert smiled, 'Are you sure you can manage with your work as well?'

'Of course we can.'

'I told her mother you would say that.' He ducked the cushion I threw.

'You had it all set up!'

He chuckled. Many times I found myself in that position. The beds stayed made up and I kept them aired. Being able to help in this way made it easier to justify our lovely home.

Having that little girl to stay was such fun. It taught me some more about this man I had married. This tough man that was such a disciplinarian was a real softy as far as little girls were concerned. As his birthday drew near Joanne and I had great fun planning our surprise. I baked a lemon sponge, she helped me make bright green icing to ice it. Then we piped white lines for a football field. She sorted out red and green jelly-babies for two teams, eating the spare ones. With royal icing we made goals over the end of a match box and a football. It was just lovely having a child around the house, it was becoming painful to us that as yet we had no children of our own. A sadistic birthday party followed where we spent the time deciding whether jelly babies should be eaten head first or nibbled from the feet up.

Robert refused to wear a watch, relying rather on his memory. He was training it as regards timekeeping he said. He was also training his mind to remember peoples' names.

'How much nicer to greet someone by name, ask for their family by name, it make them feel you care much more,' he said.

A training that always stood him in good stead.

Towser, who was to keep me company, became more and more Robert's dog, going everywhere with him. The church caretaker, Alex, and he were great friends. So while Robert counselled or wrote his sermon in the vestry, Alex and Towser would play with the enormous brush that Alex swept the hall with. The racket of Towser's barks and Alex's laughter was quite deafening at times but Robert didn't seem to notice. A very perky little dog, he defended his home and family with fearless determination, taking on allcomers to the back door as foes. Visitors to the front were greeted with a little more love. He was a dog with giant spirits despite his actual size.

At the beginning of the week Robert would start working on his sermon, and work on whatever ideas came the rest of the week. When steam was rising in the estate he did not have a minute to sit down for days on end; as happened one particular week, and he preached his best sermon. He had got into the habit of asking for my comment on the way home from church on Sundays. I gladly encouraged him when I thought it was good and tried to be gentle when correcting his grammar, which wasn't often, or saying if I thought it wasn't helpful, I knew how much work he put into it.

One Sunday after another difficult week, when travelling up Suffolk hill to home he asked the usual question.

'You're sure you want to ask me?'

He looked at me quickly, 'Yes.'

'It was rubbish,' I said quietly.

His shoulders sagged and his face lost its light.

'Other weeks when I hadn't time the Lord has undertaken for me, why not this week?'

'Maybe you had the time and didn't use it wisely,' I suggested.

I never had to say that again. In fact I rarely had to make any criticism twice, Robert took note and learnt from it.

Trying to get the garden into shape was proving difficult especially as Robert did not like helping, always finding urgent messages to be done when he saw where my inclination lay. Rather large and overgrown, the garden was going to take a lot of hard work. Robert volunteered some of the boys from the youth club to help ease his conscience. They worked with great enthusiasm, so I left them to get on with it. Some time after I heard a crack and a thud. I rushed out to find them bouncing large rocks off other large rocks.

'What are you doing?' I enquired.

'They're too big for the rockery, we're just breaking them'

I tried calmly to explain that we had nearly broken the springs in the car bringing them up from Donaghadee because they were such beautiful large stones. It took all my self-control not to cry. If they had only known how much effort it had taken to talk Robert into bringing them from 'Tara'.

'How can you be sentimental about lumps of rocks?' he asked.

'Tara' was being sold and I wanted a piece of it. Now my piece was in pieces.

I, having lost Towser to Robert, asked for a Yorkie bitch to be bought as we thought that to breed pups would be fun. The pets column was faithfully watched and an advert spotted. A girl from our youth club had decided she wanted a pup also so a whole car load of us set off to the farm near Ballynahinch. Gaily winding our way out the Saintfield Road intent on our mission, we were stopped by the police for speeding. Having given us a lecture, the policeman thankfully let us off with a caution. There were just two pups left when we arrived, a bitch and a dog. Towser picked the bitch out immediately. I had been a little anxious as to whether he would be jealous, but she took to him and he to her instantly. 'Lady Beau' settled in much faster than Towser had. Having named her we soon realised as she grew that we had named her badly. She could sit regally with her ears back and for that she got 'Victoria', but most of the time she was just a mess and 'Gipsy' would have suited her better. Finally her name was shortened to 'Boo' which stuck.

When Joanne had been re-united with her Mum now out of hospital we went on a short break to Wales. On the return boat journey from Holyhead to Dun Loaghaire we met some friends.

'We are so sorry to hear about your church.'

'Our church?' our mouths dropped open. 'What about our church?'

'It was on the news, blown up it said.'

We were into Dublin before we were able to phone and find out what had really happened. It was the wooden hall beside the church that had gone, not the new building. When we knew no-one had been hurt we were immensely relieved. The papers reporting the incident stated:

> 'The main shooting was in the Suffolk area where from mid-day yesterday until early today five hundred shots were fired at troops in the Army post at Lenadoon, the main target.'
>
> In the same area residents foiled two attempts to burn down a Methodist Church Hall at Stewartstown Road. The first attempt was at five p.m. when residents found a five gallon drum of petrol at the rear of the building. Two hours later two men and a woman were seen near the buildings and a shot was heard. When local people went to the scene, the men and girl left on foot, one of them carrying a rifle and it was discovered that the lock on the door had been broken. A second drum of petrol was found at the scene.'

They finally succeeded the next morning in blowing it up. As no windows of the new building faced that direction there was little or no damage to our church itself.

The 'Vanguard' party had emerged on the political scene and on July 21st, 1972 a press release regarding the Secretary of State, Mr William Whitelaw's talks with the IRA, was issued which stated:

> *'The IRA leaders should have been arrested and brought to
> trial when they set foot in England.'*

The English Methodist Peace Fellowship the same day were
reported in the press as having passed a resolution supporting Mr Whitelaw and also saying,

> *We welcome the promise of the introduction of proportional
> representation and assure him of the Methodist
> Conference's continued support.'*

Robert blazed with anger at these Englishmen who had no
real understanding of the problems we were living under.
They were quite prepared for us to vote under a system they
would not accept themselves. There was no comprehension
of how we lived in fear of our lives and homes every minute
of every day. They did not live as we did with callers at all
hours. We would peer from a darkened room at those callers
to see where their hands were, if their hands were in sight
and empty then all was probably OK . . ., if they were in
their pockets or inside their coats then you offered a prayer
for safety as you answered their knock, for answer you did
no matter what your fears. Some English Methodists Ministers had come over for a short time to see the situation for
themselves and some went home a little more enlightened as
to how it felt to live under such constant threat and tension.

The IRA were not getting the violent backlash they
wanted from the Protestants. In Suffolk it was mostly
because Robert had kept the lid on, so Robert had become
an actual target for the IRA snipers himself. Twice while
travelling on the estate he came under gunfire. The local
police advised that he hold a gun. After legal processes were
gone through for a gun permit, a gun was bought. Getting
used to carrying it around was difficult. Robert couldn't
reconcile it with the conviction that God was protecting
him, so it eventually ended up mostly in the house.

'I could make a mistake, think I was being shot at and
shoot some innocent person,' he said. 'Anyhow if it really
came to it, I probably wouldn't have time to use it in an
attack situation.'

The weapon became more and more rusty through neglect. I tried to clean and oil it on a couple of occasions but was never quite sure how to put it together again. Finally I gave up.

Robert came into the kitchen one day when I was preparing a meal, looking quite surprised.

'Some Roman Catholics have phoned to ask if they can come to our Bible Study.'

'What did you say?'

'I said we'd be delighted.'

'How do you think the folk will react?' I inquired.

'Our folk aren't anti-Catholic, but I will have to insist of the visitors that they pray only through our Lord Jesus, as the Bible directs, but I'll talk to them when they arrive.' There followed six months or so with these ten people who came faithfully week after week through treacherous areas, until their families, objecting to them going into a strife torn area in the dark nights, won the day and they stopped coming. Many interesting discussions took place during that time. No difficult passage of Scripture was avoided or purposely approached but differing views were openly discussed.

'People don't understand,' Robert complained to me one day. 'I would preach anywhere. If I was asked to preach in that new Anderstown Chapel I would go. Who needs to hear the gospel more that those people? I would go to Rome and to talk to the Pope, not to bow and worship him but to show him how his church and its teaching is blocking God's children from seeing their need to repent of their sins, that Jesus Christ is the only person who mediates between God and man, that God loves all his children.'

A new group of soldiers arrived in Suffolk, the Major and Lieutenants were briefed;

'Get to know the IRA Commander, the UDA Commander and Rev Robert Bradford and if you gain the confidence of those three you should have a fair idea what is going on in the estate.'

To get to Robert, one young, particularly enthusiastic Lieutenant decided to come to church and to bring his squad. A row of very uncomfortable soliders were paraded in to the back seats every Sunday. Rifles lined along the back wall of the church. They fidgeted as Robert preached of Christ his Lord and told of Calvary and they couldn't wait to get out to get their cigarettes lit up and their rifles slung over their shoulders again. A friendship blossomed with this army man although we were very aware of his purpose. A lot of prayer went up to God for that young man. One evening service finished with the Lieutenant going into the vestry to tell Robert of his dramatic conversion that week. I entered the vestry to help Robert out of his cassock, preaching bands and gowns, as was my custom, to hear our friend say,

'I thought I was completely self-sufficient.'

Our friend had stepped off the pavement of Horn Drive while patrolling, was born again as he crossed the road and stepped up the opposite pavement a different person.

Valerie, her husband Alan and ourselves were off on holiday to Italy. On the plane journey over the Alps, Robert became rather ill. In retrospect we felt the high altitude had something to do with it but at the time he became cold, grey, clammy and yet sweated profusely. A short rest in bed seemed to restore him to reasonable health and some strength and no ill effects were apparent for the remaining holiday.

Since August 1971 about five hundred Protestant families had found it necessary to move from West of Stewartstown Road area in Suffolk. This left only about one hundred Protestant families still living that Lenadoon side of the road. Twenty-two houses and flats in this Horn Drive and Doon Road area that had been left vacant had acted as a buffer zone for about six months. The decision had now been taken to allocate these houses to Roman Catholics on the Emergency Housing list. The Suffolk Tenant Association wrote to Mr Whitelaw, the then Secretary of State, asking that some Protestants be considered for these houses also to stem a further exodus of the few remaining families in that area. Robert was now taking a very active part in writing letters on behalf of the residents to Members of Parliament or other Government officials. The continued intimidation of the people was still making inroads. The threats, rattling of bin lids, whistle blowing at all hours of the day and night and window breaking were sufficient to keep everyone's nerves stretched taut. The church had been broken into three times, the Girls Brigade and Boys Brigade flags ruined and their ceremonial Union Jack stolen.

People often found their back doors knocked by children instructed by the IRA, asking when they were moving. Rubbish was dumped into the gardens, Housing Executive transfer forms were posted to people and when investigated it was originated by a phone call supposedly from the tenant himself.

Being involved with the New Vanguard Party, Robert had decided the best way of helping the situation in Ulster in general was to stand for the Northern Ireland Assembly Elections in June 1973. Robert felt he could do more in a position of power, but it was not to be. The long two weeks of campaigning in South Antrim left us feeling optimistic but with Proportional Representation, or PR, system of voting introduced, it wasn't until the fourteenth count that he was eliminated. As one dear little lady put it . . . 'I gave you twelve votes Mr Bradford' . . . She didn't appreciate it was in order of preference and she should have put a '1' at his name and not '12'. So many were confused!

The defeat was a real blow to Robert's ego as we had had high hopes. The posters on lamp-posts and walls continued to flutter in our faces for many months, turning a knife in the open wound. Humility was learnt in a costly lesson. A little book I had brought to our marriage called *Daily Light* contained quotes of Scripture for morning and evening. The reading on the morning of Saturday June 30th, 1973, the morning after the results, included:

> *'Humble yourselves therefore under the mighty hand of God, that he may exalt you in due time.'*

IN DUE TIME the Lord said. Robert accepted that as from his Maker and settled down again to parish life. As the months passed more people were coming to the services. The evening service was larger than the morning and became a real time of teaching and praise, giving the people the 'meat' of God's Word. Redemption song-books were purchased and used at these services. The choir sang gospel anthems and people were coming forward in real and total commitment of their lives to Christ.

'Politics wasn't the way,' Robert said one evening as he sat at the piano in our lounge playing his favourite hymns. I was standing behind him, my hands on his shoulders as usual, singing with him, his tenor voice singing the melody and I the alto, then without warning he would swop to singing the tenor line and I would laugh and sing the melody. We love those close times when we could shut the world out.

In October with inter-church talks under way with the Roman Catholic Church Robert launched his 'Methodist Awake' campaign. He put large advertisements in the press:

> *'METHODISTS AWAKE TO THE DANGERS . . .*
> *of dialogue with Roman Apostates;*
> *of neglecting Biblical/Wesleyan Fundamentals.*
> *Personal or congregational letters of support for a rejection of unbiblical ecumenism will be gratefully received.'*

The press picked it up. In an interview in the Belfast Telegraph in October he stated:

> *'I believe I am speaking for thousands of grass-roots Methodists who were never consulted about these talks. A referendum of each congregation should be taken. My aim is to get the voice of the ordinary Methodists heard at the next conference. I am not opposed to talks with Roman Catholics on social issues like drug abuse, but talking with them on other matters is futile. The dogmatic stance of the Catholic hierarchy can never be altered. I believe that talking to Roman Catholics at the home level on theology is acceptable, for I feel a genuine concern that the grass-roots Catholic is being deluded and misled by the church hierarchy.'*

Determined to try to change our church from within he added:

> *'I am fighting to save the Methodist Church as laid down by our documents of faith, it is the Talk Supporters who have strayed from the official position.'*

A series of letters appeared in the press, both supportive and abusive, letters to us personally again supportive and abusive. A real campaign of bitter phone calls began, often leaving me weak and weeping or just plain angry. But the tremendous response from the Methodist people themselves made Robert press on. The terrorists stepped up their campaign in Suffolk and life in the estate was lived at a high level of tension. It is not possible to live normally in the midst of a terrorist war but the people tried. Army patrolled the area constantly, if you jumped a garden fence you might have found yourself tripping over the prone form of a soldier on watch, the rest of the patrol around various corners and under other hedges nearby. As you drove around at night if a patrol came into your headlights you turned them off and drove by sidelights for fear of them being picked off by the ever-present snipers.

The church leaders wrote again to the Secretary of State, Mr William Whitelaw, to ask for greater protection for our church buildings. The army in the area were doing their best for us but were stretched very thin.

> '*May we stress once again the fears of our people, for we believe that the attacks on our Church have been designed to undermine the confidence of our people, and thereby make them lose hope for the future. If this happens it may well be that we will have another exodus of Protestant people from the area and we believe this is what the IRA wants.*'

With the constant struggle to live normally despite severe intimidations, windows being constantly broken, bomb scares meaning the women spent hours standing in the street unable to shop or to get home, the worry of children being taught violence at an early age because of the environment in which they lived, we felt more than ever that the Lord had sent us to this area. This was our mission field. We didn't have to cross any water to fight for right and justice in a heathen land: we had all that in Suffolk.

It is well the Good Lord does not allow us to know all that is in front of us for there were to be changed days ahead.

4

Fostering pre-adoption babies was fun and when Boo produced a litter of six pups it was just lovely. Our home rocked with the cries of babies and puppies yelping and for the first time that large house seemed full. But with time they were all gone again. I decided to go back to work, this time in Musgrave Park Orthopaedic Theatre, a whole new sphere for me. We had high hopes that this year of 1974 would see great strides in our little church and the dawn of new hope for Suffolk.

A deputation arrived one Monday to see Robert, I showed them into the lounge and offered them a cup of coffee or tea, then fetched him from his sermon preparation in the upstairs study.

'They want me to stand as an Anti-Sunningdale Candidate in the forthcoming Parliamentary Elections,' Robert told me afterwards.

I glanced at him quickly, rather apprehensive.

'It's all right,' he smiled, 'I told them I wasn't even slightly interested.'

Then he frowned. 'They are coming back on Friday.'

'What for?' I asked apprehensive again.

'They think I'll change my mind,' he smiled.

'Will you?'

'No.'

Tuesday came and Robert was looking rather anxious, Wednesday the same, by Thursday he was like a caged lion.

'What's wrong?' I finally asked in exasperation.

'I was so sure my defeat in Assembly elections was a sign that I wasn't to go into politics. I've prayed about this expecting an instant "No", but I can't get it. Neither can I get a definite "Yes" I don't know where I am, or what I'm supposed to do. It would be awful to stand again, this time knowing I can't win, to go through another humiliating defeat just for the principle of letting people vote to show their disapproval of the talks at Sunningdale.'

At that time Robert was reading a little book by Derick Bingham called *Admidst Alien Corn*, a study of the Book of Ruth. Mr Bingham had written.

'The greatest guiding line to follow when faced with a decision as a Christian is to shut your door. Get the influences of life out of the way and explain everything in secret to your heavenly Father. Acknowledge him. Then go and act in a common sense manner according to your abilities and limitations. When you acknowledge him, he then directs your paths. Ask two simple questions, "Is it right?" and "Is it necessary?" If there is no cloud between you and your Lord, go ahead.'

Robert had acknowledged the Lord, it was only if it was God's will that he was prepared to take on this task. Was it right? He felt it was right to give people the chance to vote to show their disapproval of what the present elected jepresentatives were doing. Was it necessary for him? All other three candidates had said that if Robert stood they would stand down, an unheard-of precedent in politics! Yet, Robert still wasn't totally convinced.

The delegation called again and that day it was a very subdued Robert that greeted them.

'I can't say "Yes" but I can't either give you a definite "No." When must you definitely know?'

Saturday night was the deadline. A meeting of all candidates was to be held in Bill Craig's house and they would need his answer then.

He walked down the stairs on Friday looking quite smug.

'Come to a decision?' I ventured from the kitchen.

'I've done something I've never done before and probably will never do again, I've put a fleece down for the Lord.'

'Pardon?' I said, not quite believing and more than a little surprised.

He chuckled, 'I've put a fleece down, you know the Old Testament . . .'

'I know what a fleece is,' I interrupted impatiently.

'Well it suddenly struck me that it costs a lot of money to fight an election campaign, and as we are permanently in the red in the bank, we can't provide it. So I asked God to provide the one thousand pounds we'll need, if he wants me to stand.'

He was still smiling when the telephone rang beside him in the hall alcove under the stairs. His end of the conversation was monosyllabic, but his face had drained of all colour. I put on the kettle as he listened on the phone. He replaced the receiver and went into the dining-room. I found him sitting hunched in a rocking chair staring into the blazing fire. I handed him the coffee.

'Bad news?' I ventured.

'That was a call to tell me there's an anonymous gentleman who'll back me to the tune of one thousand pounds if I will "stand".'

It was my turn to sit down quickly. We both sat quietly for a long time letting the significance of it all sink in. Then Robert began to think out loud.

'If I stand and lose there's the humiliation, even though I'm prepared for it. If by some strange quirk we won, then where would I be? Would we have to leave Suffolk? Or could I do both jobs? The church would be bound to suffer because I wouldn't be able to spend anything like the same time on visitation. I would be in London for a large part of the week. But if that's how I'm being led by God, I have to do it. Everything is so good in the church just now I can't believe it's all to change.'

Robert seemed like a stranger prowling round the house for the next twenty-four hours. I was praying so hard that he would be shown clearly what to do and make the right decision. Finally the time came to leave for Bill Craig's house.

'Come with me love?' he asked. In the car he drove slowly and silently. I didn't speak either. When we drove into Bill Craig's driveway he stopped the car and just sat.

'You have to decide,' I urged, 'all the signs are there that you are to do it.'

'I know, but I don't want to.' He slowly opened the car door and went towards the house. I waited in the car, still praying and slowly freezing. Inside the men were gathered around the dining-room table. Robert sat down quietly and the inevitable question was asked.

'Will you do it?'

'No, I . . .' said Robert.

But no-one heard him! The chandelier above their heads had given a loud crack at that precise moment and everyone looked up. Knowing that it was God overriding his decision, Robert quickly said, 'Yes, yes, I'll do it.'

The group were jubilant and planning began in earnest

with Robert spending most of the evening glancing at the chandelier and wondering what his Saviour had in store for him. He hoped our leaders and people in Suffolk would understand, but he shouldn't have worried.

The United Ulster Unionist Council, or the UUUC, was a combination of Mr Harry West's Unionists, Mr William Craig's Vanguard Unionists and the Dr Ian Paisley's Democratic Unionists, all banded together as UUUC to give an Anti-Sunningdale platform for the election and the battle was on for real. Trevor Harvey, the printer, worked night and day to produce leaflets and posters for the campaign. Raymond Jordan, Robert's election agent, worked from midnight until morning producing the goods for his home bakery, then spent all day organising the campaign without any sleep. Finally the leaflets arrived . . .

> ROBERT BRADFORD   X   (FOR SOUTH BELFAST)
> UNITY WITH GREAT BRITAIN
> UNITY OF ALL TRADITIONAL UNIONISTS
> UNITY FOR THE DEFEAT OF VIOLENCE
> UNITY AGAINST THE COUNCIL OF IRELAND

The Belfast Telegraph on 20th February read:

'NOW, POUNDER IS ALL SET TO MAKE IT A FIVE TIMER'.

The paper gave a synopsis of the five candidates with photos and included an article on how Mr Pounder would easily win again. Just eight days to go and tension was mounting. Every house in the constituency had its door knocked on and leaflets were handed in, that is every door except those in staunch Republican areas where it was not safe to venture. Teams of people gathered every night and with car loads of literature went in their various designated directions. Tramping the streets night after night in dark cold February was not my idea of fun. But as more and more people said they were voting our way, our hopes began to rise. I even surprised myself by doing a bit of electioneering amongst the surgeons at work. The big breakthrough of the campaign happened one night when Bill Craig allowed Robert to take his place on a TV debate amongst the candidates. As we knocked doors that night we asked people to watch and judge for themselves. People were obviously impressed with Robert's ability to speak his mind concisely and well. He was sure of his facts, articulate and polite to his opponents, and immaculate in appearance.

As Thursday 28th February drew near we began to get really excited. There was such a tremendous reaction over all South Belfast to our campaign of visitation and posted literature, that at our late evening get-togethers in the Jordans' home we began to feel we really had a chance of not just getting an Anti-Sunningdale vote but actually winning the seat.

As I tramped the streets night after night listening to the various snippets of conversation from various groups of people I found myself in a different world. I began to realise what a sheltered life I had led until now. I hadn't realised how much people had refrained from swearing in my presence, how much the conversation had been toned down for my benefit. The shattering experiences of knocking on doors and being sworn at, having the door slammed in my face, or threats of having dogs set on me, were all new to me. The groups were very protective of me but it was impossible to judge by the look of a house what sort of reaction to expect at the door. Whether grand or small you were sure of a mixed reaction.

The 28th arrived and Robert and Raymond had an excellent plan organised to cover all the polling stations. The phones were manned constantly and they buzzed all day with people needing help of various kinds. The cars with loud-speakers went around encouraging people to come out and vote in areas that we were afraid would have a low turn out. In one area Robert set up an account with a fish and chip shop to feed any of our workers that came in, and packets of the same or sandwiches were distributed by Robert and Raymond to the various people at polling stations along with flasks of coffee. standing at one of these locations I was very thankful for it, it was so bitterly cold. I offered some to my opponent, a lady giving out Alliance Party leaflets. She looked at me in amazement and took some very reticently. I wondered, did she think I was going to poison her! A very stilted conversation ensued, then we took up our opposing positions on either side of the gate.

Finally the polling stations were to close and Robert had designated me as his representative to watch that the boxes were sealed properly. One of the boxes was being left quite loose and I pointed it out.

'It might be to your advantage,' the man whispered urgently looking round him. I was furious! I couldn't understand this attitude about elections, that anything goes.

'All's fair in love and war,' I was quoted again and again, 'and this is definitely war!' they would add.

It seemed amazing that this was the end. The last ten days had been like a dream. Very little sleep was had by anyone as we sat up till the small hours each evening going over the day's events. The funny incidents being recounted time and again and as each new group arrived in they added theirs. Tonight it was the accounts of the Polling Day. One of our workers at a Polling Station in Einaghy had become so confident of victory that instead of handing out the leaflets with Robert's picture and a short synopsis of what he was standing for, he was heard saying 'Get your souvenir picture of the winner here, get your souvenir picture of your new MP now!'

'If we're to win, it will be because the Lord wants us to, or if we lose it's in his plan. Let's leave it in the Lord's hands,' Robert commented on the way home when the day was over. 'But if we've won it's going to change our lives drastically.'

We had talked this over lightly during the last ten days but now the results seemed certain, we were both a little apprehensive.

'The hierarchy of the Methodist Church aren't going to like it,' I said.

'Well they've got Lord Soper in the English Church in Parliament, they'll just have to come to terms with it.'

Raymond and Billy McAllister had been down at the count in Belfast City Hall from the start. At nine o'clock they phoned us as we were getting organised to leave home. 'We really think you'll make it!' Raymond and Billy were very excited.

'They've opened some of the boxes from the staunch Republican areas and you are getting an amazing number of Roman Catholic votes'.

Robert went and finished shaving, singing lustily as he

went, ducked his head in cold water as was his habit and dragged his hair flat before carefully encouraging each wave into place. I was ready long before him and waiting very impatiently.

'We'll be sitting down there for hours love,' he smiled at me as we finally got into the car.

The City Hall is a very impressive building but that day I noticed little of it. We tried to walk unconcerned up the marble stairway and along the interminable corridors. The noise of voices was deafening but as we entered the large hall where the South Belfast count was under way the atmosphere was strangely hushed. The counters were seated on the inside of two sets of long tables facing out to the front and side of the platform. The first few sorting votes into piles for pigeon holes with the various candidates names on them, the next lot resorting in case of mistakes and counting and the rest doing the final counting. The whole procedure was being carefully scrutinised by the various candidates and their agents. The efficiency of it hit me immediately. On the centre table were the finished piles of voting papers carefully elasticated together in one-thousands. It was at this stage obviously a very close battle between Rafton Pounder and Robert. As different boxes were opened Mr Pounder would go ahead by a thousand then we would be two thousand ahead, then he would catch up again. As the hours ticked by and we increased our lead, the tension was at nail-biting pitch. A strained cordiality broke out between the candidates now that the battle was almost over. It was almost noon when Mr Pounder came over and shook Robert's hand.

'I think you've made it, congratulations.'

What a gentleman, I thought; and have we really won? It surely wasn't possible!

The hush had gone, the tables were being moved and everyone was chattering excitedly and I was being pushed to the front beside Robert. The press arch lights were trained on the Presiding Officer, microphone in hand the TV cameras were turning. His voice boomed out with the results in alphabetical order. Robert Bradford . . . 22,083. A yell of delight went up and quickly stilled. Rafton Pounder . . . 18,085. At that point I thought the roof was going to come off. Silence was requested and he continued. Robert then spoke expressing his thanks to all concerned and I stood dazed watching. What in the world did the future hold now? I didn't dare think. It was over and Robert was carried shoulder high through the crowd and I had to fight to stay with him. The TV interviews were quickly over and shoulder high again he was out in the street.

'I made a fortune on you to-day Sir,' a little man yelled over the crowd. 'I'm only sorry I didn't get my money on when you were a hundred to one instead of just thirty-three to one!' Saturday's papers all carried photos and long accounts of the previous day's amazing events. The UUUC had captured eleven of the twelve seats. But it was one particular photo of us in the Belfast News Letter that caught my eye. There was a smudge on the picture just like a bullet-hole on Robert's forehead. I commented on it in Raymond's house and the others quickly said, 'Oh it will only be that copy, Norah, just a smudge of ink.'

We picked up the other copies and went through them. Sure enough it was there on every copy in every edition. An ominous shiver went down my spine that I couldn't shake off.

The victory car cavalcade around South Belfast was great fun and a real release of tension with posters Raymond had got printed strung to the cars with 'NICE ONE ROBERT,' his photo in the centre and the number of votes underneath.

Our people in Suffolk had been very much with us in this election as Robert had gone to great lengths to explain to them his reasons. So the leaders were organised to undertake the visiting of parishioners to ease Robert's load, and they seemed happy to undertake the task.

The airport was only half an hour from Suffolk but Robert couldn't get used to the fact that although it was only an hour's plane trip to London it was at least three and a half hours to Westminister if everything connected. Then there were the hold-ups of fog, ice or snow, plane delays for all sorts of mechanical reasons.

Westminster Palace where the House of Commons and the House of Lords sits is a world of its own. Its pomp and ceremony greets you as you come in any of the great entrances. Even the policemen are more sedate and there is a general sense of awe. I couldn't wait to be able to see it for myself. That day came around and Robert phoned to see if I was all set.

'I have to bank your pay cheque, then I'll be on my way.'

'Don't bank it, cash it and bring it with you. What the bank manager doesn't see won't worry him! We'll be able to go to a nice show and have a meal or two out.'

Our bank balance was definitely still in technicolour, though hopefully not for too much longer.

It was going to be such fun to be there for Robert's Maiden Speech to that Grand House of Commons. I visualised the packed seats with everyone in rapt attention to Robert's every word. Instead there were a total of about thirty members lazing half asleep in the studded green leather, oak panelled pews. It is an unwritten rule in Westminster that you don't pick holes in Maiden Speeches. Such was not to be the case for Robert, he was thrown in at the deep end. Robert began . . .

> *'I believe that it is customary for an Hon. Member making a Maiden Speech to indulge in some pleasantries, but such is the grave situation in Northern Ireland that I shall have to set these pleasantries aside and get down to the facts . . .'*

He went on to talk of South Belfast and asked:

> *'When will this Hon. House give the British Army – our Army – and the Royal Ulster Constabulary the freedom which they need to deal fully and completely with terrorism? The second question which our folk are asking is when the British Government will cease deliberately to miss the point. It is not enough to align the UDA and the UVF and the IRA. It is not enough to state that the Protestant extremists are as bad as the Republican extremists. We deplore any man who bombs, kills or shoots in our name. He does not fight our battle. But we must remember that the violence and the terrorism began with the IRA. It continues under the clear auspices of that movement and because of the ineptitude of this House and of the forces under strict political control there was reaction.'*

Robert went on to talk of the Constitution Act as being undemocratic.

'*For example there was a refusal to accept power sharing in this House but for the Ulster people it is regarded as being the only answer. The great Lion of Judah has brought forth a subtle slimy snake called Sunningdale, and we are asked to accept that this is British Democracy. I think that the root cause of the confusion is the fact that in Northern Ireland there is an attempt by aspirants and supporters of one sovereign State to disinherit another sovereign State. This Honourable House would never conceive of a time when, If there were enough of them, the Pakistanis here would declare that this Island, because they had a majority, should become a colony of Pakistan; Ulster is British. Ulster wishes to remain British. Ulster does not want to be disinherited and will not be disinherited. I had hoped that the Labour Government would indulge in honest, open government. They made that claim. They have promised the country, and rightly so, to look again at the EEC membership into which we were dragged without the consultation which had been promised. They have said that they will look for the mind of the United Kingdom on that issue. Why then are the Government denying the Ulster people precisely the same right to express their opinion on a matter which is so very dear to our hearts, our continued membership of this wonderful historic nation? We ask for nothing more than to be permitted to remain British and to have that status safeguarded not by devious documents called the Constitution Act, but in clear, explicit terms which can and must and, I trust, will go from this Honourable House. There are faithful sons and daughters in Ulster tonight who are waiting for the return of a prodigal mother.*'

Robert sat down.

Mr Duffy, the Member for Sheffield, Attercliffe stood up.

'*The Honourable Member for Belfast South disclaimed at the outset of his Maiden speech his intention to call in aid the courtesies and conventions of the House. I wish I could call them in aid in following him. I think that you in your charity, Mr Deputy Speaker, would at least expect me to welcome him to this Honourable House but I hope you will accept that it would require a deranged sense of generosity,*

93

> *not only on my part but on the part of many other Honourable Members for me to compliment the Honourable Member on his speech.'*

And so the scene was set. Robert was aware of the battle he was engaged in and plunged in with all his energy.

This Labour Government had the slimmest of majorities and therefore the weight of the eleven Northern Ireland Members votes were sought on many issues. The UUUC team worked closely on this and used strategy. Sometimes a better point was made by abstaining than by voting at all. But to abstain you had to be in the House to be counted as abstaining.

Back home, several letters were printed in the papers objecting to Robert wearing his clerical collar during the election. For the first time I was tempted to answer those complaints myself. The truth of the matter was Robert only possessed two non-clerical shirts and ties, and when they were in the wash he was reduced to clerical collar whether he wanted to or not. Robert replied to the various criticisms stating with regard to his congregation that he had decided to ask to enter the 'Sector Ministry' when his term at Suffolk was completed. 'The Sector Ministry simply means,' he stated, 'that one expresses one's spiritual moral awareness in the wider community without having pastoral responsibilities for a particular congregation. I shall reside in the constituency and preach the Gospel in it whenever the opportunities present themselves. Another important consideration is that a Christian Minister in Parliament can help to formulate and implement 'moral' legislation and in doing this achieves something which is normally beyond the influence of the parish minister. There is therefore the argument that prevention is better than cure and if we had had more Christians in Parliament we would have less questionable legislation.'

The IRA terrorists went into full swing with its campaign of enticing policemen into traps, and so began a new phase of this war. Two policemen were gunned down in Dunmurry near our manse.

'The killing of these loyal servants of the community is too infuriating for words' Robert said, 'all decent men will demand the ruthless pursuit of the murderers until they are

94

brought to justice. How many more deaths must occur before Westminster stops playing politics with Ulster's Blood?'

In April a serious situation had developed and Ulster found itself in the middle of a Loyalist Workers Strike. Many politicians tried to negotiate to get the men back to work, feeling the time was not right for such a drastic move, but Ulster had had enough. Robert appealed in the press:

'There is still real hope of political progress.'

Mr Merlyn Rees, now the Secretary of State for Northern Ireland, was then reported as sticking to his attitude that he was not prepared to enter into negotiations with the strikers. The strikers, it was reported by Northern Ireland Office, did not turn up for the meeting. Whatever the truth the situation was stalemate, that was until Mr Harold Wilson, the Prime Minister, made his now infamous speech and referred to the people of Ulster as 'Spongers.'

Ulster rose *'en masse'* in fury and the strike began in earnest with the politicians backing it. Electricity was cut off for longer and longer periods, except in areas including a hospital, though there also sometimes. Food began to be in short supply as shops joined in. Petrol and other supplies weren't getting through the road blocks that were set up and manned by Loyalist workers. On the whole these blocks remained peaceful unless someone they didn't regard as an essential worker tried to get through. Nurses, doctors and other essential workers had to produce identification to get through. Ulster slowly ground to a halt. The farmers were perhaps the ones to suffer the most financially as they lost whole batches of chickens and other livestock without the necessary heat. In hospital life became very difficult. Because of the design of their back-up generator systems many were unable to use their operating theatres. Musgrave Park Hospital where I worked was one such case. If the electricity went off during an operation the change over to our own generators would have produced a cloud of dust which meant we could only do emergency work.

After a long day of sitting knitting and waiting for emergency work I arrived home to find Robert in the dining-room trying to cook some food for us. He had lit the fire and was sitting with a saucepan on it heating up some processed peas. Beside him he had another can of stewed meat and another of new potatoes. The whole scene looked so unappetising that my hunger left me. I managed to persuade him finally that if we put them all together in one large saucepan at least they would all be hot together. Towser and Boo ate well that night! Opponents of the strike had a hard time as they were prevented from getting to or from their work. We found battery radio was the surest form of communication as the electricity cut-offs means we couldn't depend on the TV for news.

In the estates around South Belfast as in many parts of Ulster a system was worked out to ensure that no elderly person suffered. Milk and coal were distributed to them. Camping apparatus was hauled out of attics and caravans and put to use in the homes.

The Ulster Workers Council were calling for early Assembly elections and the scrapping of the Sunningdale agreement, which we had thought would have been automatic after the Westminster elections of February and the massive Ulster 421,782 anti-Sunningdale talks vote to 295,858 pro-Sunningdale talks. Finally the Executive at Stormont fell and the strike ended with rejoicing and celebrations. Hillsborough farmers headed one celebration cavalcade with a trailer containing three donkeys called, Gerry Paddy and Brian, supposedly representing the leaders of the defeated coalition parties.

The Methodist Church conference in June was to be held in Cork. Knowing it was going to be a very rough ride for Robert I arranged some time off work and went along.

As we had to travel through the Republic of Ireland to get to Conference, arrangements had been made to give us a Guarda escort. This made life rather difficult for us as we couldn't hurry and as usual we were late. As we travelled from area to area out Guarda escort changed. By the third or fourth set we were very late but resigned that we couldn't alter the situation. Our latest Guarda companions flagged us down.

'You're rather late Sir,' he said, saluting as Robert wound the window down.

'Yes, I'm afraid so.' Robert tried not to sound impatient.

'We are going to hit a lot of traffic from here on, keep

tight on our tail and we'll see if we can't get you through.'

With that we started up again, with them in front now. Headlights full on, siren blazing, they proceeded up the centre of the road. The traffic parted like the waves of the Red Sea so we stuck to them like glue and in no time at all we were through what would have been a real bottleneck. It was fun.

Arriving in Cork City I dropped Robert at Wesley Chapel where Conference was being held and proceeded to the boarding house that Conference had allocated us to. The slight middle-aged lady who answered the door to me preceeded me up the narrow hall to her dining-room wringing her hands.

'There's a mistake,' her eyes were frightened, 'I told them that I couldn't have the Guarda guarding the house – bad for business you know. You understand?'

She was miserably shifting from foot to foot wringing her hands in her anxiety to persuade me to go.

'They should have told you, not let you come on out.'

I tried to explain that I hadn't gone into Conference but she wasn't listening, so I picked up the cases and made for the door. She was obviously terrified that her house would be a target for the IRA, and I felt terribly sorry for her.

As the week went on Robert became more and more alienated from his colleagues. They didn't seem to want to know about his Methodists Awake Campaign and the eight-thousand Methodist signatures of support.

I sat in on some sessions, other times when the discussion was uninteresting to me, I shopped or went and sunbathed on a local beach. The Guarda stayed on duty at Wesley Chapel while Robert was inside. I got rather irritated at finding them constantly asleep so when I picked Robert up at five o'clock one evening for a trip out west I decided I would waken them. I took off through the traffic like a rocket without even waiting to see if they had noticed our departure. It was rush hour. Robert's definition of Southern Irish taxi drivers was that to get a license in Dublin they had to cause five accidents but to get a license in Cork they had to cause ten! According to Robert I was doing even better than them. I wove in and out of the traffic, changed lanes often and gave them a terrible time. Once out of town I had to ease up as there was no traffic. Our friends whom we intended to visit lived right in the heart of the countryside down a maze of lanes. These lanes were totally devoid of signposts and unless you knew your way there were not even road names to go by and a stranger could easily get lost. I knew my way well and sped around the lanes knowing each pothole and bad curve. When we reached the farm our escort climbed out of their car rather slowly. Robert went over to speak with them and I lingered within earshot. 'You'll be fine here Mr Bradford, will you be wanting to leave before a couple of hours?' the plain clothes policeman said in his lilting Cork brogue. Robert said no and after laughing with them about the terrible time I'd given them, he turned towards the house.

'Excuse me, your Reverence,' the policeman looked rather sheepish, 'could you tell me how to get to Clonikilty from here?'

Robert restrained his laughter and directed them. Later that night for some reason, he insisted on driving back.

As the days passed it became obvious that the ecumenical trend within the church was so strong that Robert was battering his head against a brick wall. We came home feeling totally isolated from a church that had been our foundation.

Our days in the Irish Methodist Church had come to an end. We were home barely a month when Robert's resignation was in the hands of the hierarchy. Then began the speculation in the press as to what we would do. Would we join the Dr Ian Paisley's church? Many thought so. Would we start a new sect? What had Robert in mind? Robert stated in the press:

> 'There are irreconcilable differences between me and the leadership, particularly on the ecumenical movement and the current political situation.'

He stated he would not be joining Mr Paisley's church.

'I am a Methodist and will always remain a Methodist Minister. I am going to the United States later this year with a view to becoming associated with a Methodist Conference which would enable me to continue preaching Methodism in Ulster.' We had discovered to our dismay that Robert's ordination as a Methodist Minister could be removed if he did not hold a weekly meeting and that being his only qualification we were very fearful for the future. Another election was looming large on the horizon and Robert wondered whether he would fall between two stools.

'We could always emigrate,' he would tease.

At that point I would have gladly lived anywhere but Ulster but I knew God had placed us in the position we were in to teach us to lean on him. Our congregation were still with us and they lavished love on us.

As we began to think seriously about setting up our own home elsewhere I counted up our main possessions, they consisted of two rocking chairs, a fridge, a washing machine, a double bed and a hearth rug. Many people have much less, I consoled myself, but not usually after four years of married life. Not muct to set up a new home with. Robert approached the Housing Executive about renting a flat, knowing the only place we could get accommodation to rent quickly was in Suffolk. We had to be out of the manse by the end of August so we went on to the Emergency List. No-one wanted to live in Suffolk, so our chances were good.

Robert and I packed our bits and pieces and waited for news. The hardest thing for Robert was packing his precious books.

'We will only have room for one box in the flat so keep you most needed ones together.'

This was asking the impossible but it was finally done. Robert was off to America with some vague addresses to contact some Methodist Churches in the Southern States of Mississippi and Louisiana.

I was terrified at being left as I would perhaps have to move house before his return.

Landing in Jackson, Mississippi, Robert was met by Rev Ben Gerald, the then President of the Mississippi Conference of the Methodist Protestant Church. Mr Gerald took Robert to his home and then to whichever churches he wanted to visit. Nothing was too much trouble for this gentleman yet he put no pressure on Robert. Robert found there was an affinity between himself and Ben's people, so he decided that if they would have him, he would join. To celebrate, an evening meal out was arranged for Robert and various ministers and dignitaries of the church. They were all seated around a large table chatting, enjoying their new-found friendship and the waitress was working her way round the table taking each person's order. She came to Robert and with a straight face he ordered his meal and a double brandy. There was a rapid stunned silence; Rev Brand Kenkins' mouth dropped open. Robert pretended not to notice and continued talking until his laughter errupted at the sight of all their shocked faces.

'Cancel that order,' Robert called to the waitress who couldn't have served him in that teetotal restaurant anyhow. The table was rocking with laughter with Robert and Brand wiping the tears from their eyes.

'You should have seen your faces,' Robert roared.

'I was sure wondering about you my friend,' said Brand when he had recovered sufficiently to speak.

Back home the Housing Executive notified me of a vacant two-bedroom flat and rather apprehensively I collected the keys and went to see it. It was a first-floor flat on a corner with just one other flat below it. The main problem was that it looked directly into the Ladybrook Roman Catholic estate and the chance of a sniper attack was very real. I asked the police for advice and they felt, as I did, that anywhere in Suffolk was dangerous and we were taking a chance. They promised to get the bullet-proofing done to doors and windows as quickly as possible so I told the Housing Executive I would take it.

The flat colour scheme was not to my liking so I decided to do some painting before moving in as I still had a few days to spare. So my friends Christine and Brian came with paint-pots and brushes in hand and we slapped a coat of fresh-smelling paint over all the walls. I consoled myself that it was only for six months when we hoped to have enough money saved to put a deposit on a permanent home. The rise in salary from approximately one thousand pounds per annum as a cleric to four and a half thousand as an MP seemed enormous to us and I felt we would soon be in a position to buy our own home.

Robert arrived home jubilant about his new-found friends. 'They're "true blue" Methodist, very evangelical and on top of that they are just very nice people. God has really prospered their church through adversity.' With regard to the flat he wasn't so keen, but he realised I had had little option. He amazingly decided to help with the painting. I gladly gave him a brush and a pot of paint and watched out of the corner of my eye as I worked. The heavy embossed paper in the lounge we were painting was very hard to cover and he soon gave up, deciding he had an urgent message to do. The shocking pink colour showed through unless you attacked it with the brush at many different angles. One wall was to be moss-green with the rest of the lounge white. If I had realised what a dark north facing room it was I would have chosen differently. I had managed to purchase a very comfortable three-piece suite for one hundred and sixty-eight pounds and an electric cooker but it would be some time before we could order carpets and get them laid. Our new home was taking shape. That we would own all the furnishings was a lovely thought. In the manse if we scratched or broke anything there was the awful feeling that we would have to replace it or own up to it when moving.

The Suffolk congregation arranged a farewell evening for us. It was such a lovely night with many musical items by the choir and soloists secretly rehearsed. As the presentations began, organisation by organisation came forward. I was overwhelmed. The choir presented me with a gold watch. The Girls' Brigade with an electric lamp, the Women's Department with a double-bed duvet and so on. It seemed endless. Robert was presented with a cheque for a hundred pounds and a special Scout Award called a 'Thanks' badge. It became a treasured possession which he wore proudly. The Rev Day Ludlow, a supernumery minister on the circuit, was introducing the items. Then Robert spoke. I don't remember much of what he said as I tried to fight back the tears. My mind wandered back to the times we'd had together. Such blessings from our God had been lavished upon us in Suffolk in souls gained for our Saviour; in true friendship and wonderful times of fellowship and praise. I thought of the young people who we had managed to draw away from drink, drugs and even witchcraft, and then see them replace that with Christ in their lives. I thought of the nights with my Women's Department when time and again speakers booked would phone to say they couldn't come. How those long-suffering ladies were treated time and again to our holiday slides or me trying to sing with my guitar, or a Bible quizz or whatever I could think up at the last minute! I winced at the memory. I remembered the funny things too, like the day Robert had met the boys from Suffolk football team just after they had won the churches' league.

'I'm going to put aside my principles,' Robert announced while standing talking to them. 'Everyone down to the *Black Swan* in Dunmurry, the drinks are on me!

Well, no-one believed him.

'Are you really serious Vicar?'

Eventually they all piled into their cars and sped off in the direction of Dunmurry, Robert following unable to keep from grinning. They arrived on the scene to find the pub a heap of rubble with the dust hardly settled where the *Black Swan* had stood.

'Would you look at that,' said Robert in mock amazement, 'that's God's judgement on me for thinking of dropping my principles.' He drove off quickly before they could lynch him. He had been past just after the bomb had gone off knew no-one had been hurt and thought it was unlikely to have been on the news yet. He never could resist a good joke.

On Saturdays, evenings on the way home after the youth club, Robert would sometimes stop at the British Legion Hall and run in for a minute. Many would choke on their beer as he appeared, much to his amusement. His purpose was to get to know many of his congregation who worked long hours and encourage their church attendance. 'Christ died for sinners,' he would say to me as he bounced back into the car. It paid off, some started coming on Sundays.

I thought how our church members who have moved had fanned out across the world to New Zealand, Australia and England; we were almost like a Missionary society sending ambassadors for our King, and now our part in those proceedings was at an end. I wiped my eyes and became conscious of Robert's voice as he finished.

'Don't rember Robert – remember rather Robert Bradford's Saviour.' He sat down beside me very pale, I knew he was finding it as hard as I was, harder even, if that were possible. Mr Ludlow re-iterated Robert's comments and added some kindly ones of his own in his gentle sincere way and the proceedings drew to a close.

Robert ended with his own benediction, 'And now may the grace of the Lord Jesus Christ, the love of God and the friendship of the Holy Spirit be with you all now and until Christ comes or calls.'

We walked out of that beautiful building with very heavy hearts. We knew that though living only around the corner we would not be able to attend services. The Methodists' unwritten rule that you don't go back to your previous church for a year to allow a new man to settle in, definitely applied to us. Anyone might find it difficult following Robert in the normal circumstances because he always threw himself one hundred per cent into anything he did and because of the sheer volume of work he got through. The fact that he was practically regarded as a patron saint in the area would make it an impossible task, and one that we were not going to make any more difficult. It was only to be a matter of days before we moved to the flat in the back of a van borrowed from a local Roman Catholic shopkeeper. Then we would have to shut our door on all the problems around and stay aloof. A very difficult task when we cared so much.

A new era was about to begin for us – and not a very pleasant one.

5

The flat was terribly noisy. We had no carpets for the first while, so every sound seemed to echo and the dogs, unused to the constant traffic and general noise, seemed to bark continually. I had visions of the Housing Executive evicting us. I felt so sorry for our neighbours who had to put up with us. The worst came at night. With our flat being on a corner and the garden having been allowed to grow wild, every dog in the neighbourhood seemed to congregate there and have gang warfare. Almost every night we were woken with growlings and snarlings of yet another dog fight as they fought to see who was king of the pack.

It seemed we hardly had our feet on the ground when another election was called. There had been so much bad publicity about our departure from the church that we wondered how the public would react when it came to voting. A priority during the last few months had been to buy two new suits for Robert because his black clerical suits seemed our of place, and some new shirts and ties.

'At least we won't have people complaining about his clerical collar this time,' I thought.

This election was fought with a different emphasis. Robert summed it up for a press release:

> 'The Constitution must be secured with full parity with the rest of the United Kingdom assured. Second, this basic right of United Kingdom citizenship must be safeguarded by a determined security policy which will isolate and root out the terrorist. Third, the industrial and social problems must be tackled forcibly, especially the chronic housing shortage, to which I have given much of my time. Fourth, a realistic and lasting peace must be sought enabling every law-abiding citizen, irrespective of religion, the right to enjoy our province.'

A big boost came to the UUUC when the Right Honourable Enoch Powell joined the ranks to fight for the cause and stand for election in South Down. Polling Day was Thursday October 10th 1974. By the time polls were closed we were very confident of victory and very relieved that perhaps for the next while Robert had a job.

South Belfast count was generally first to be called out with West Belfast close on its heels. With an electorate of 75,443 Robert had gained an increase to 30,116 votes. He took the opportunity to blast the press for what he felt was their unfair treatment of him. That was a big mistake, as he was to find. Politicians depend immensely on the press, if they are not quoted in the paper, seen on TV or heard on the radio, the general public assume they are not working.

A battle developed then with the press joining ranks to ignore him. He could not get TV coverage, his press-releases were lost amongst the pages or ignored. All in all Robert was the loser. It was months before they forgave him, and he realised whether he liked it or not, in public life he would have to woo the press.

The Westminster soccer team selected Robert to play for them. Robert was thrilled because he was finding the change of physical pace at Westminster a difficult transition. To sit on those green leather benches and listen to speeches for six to ten hours, often until many hours into the morning was so much of a change that it was difficult to adjust and he was putting on weight.

Further adjustment was necessary on Sundays: instead of preaching, we found ourselves with no set church to attend. Choosing where and going to church together was a new-found pleasure. We had sat together rarely since we were married and it felt good.

We could not find one particular church that we wanted to link up with. Robert liked the Presbyterian preaching: 'real meat' he would say. I couldn't cope with what I felt was their massacre of some beautiful hymns by the speed they were sung at. The Baptist church in Great Victoria Street suited us better. But when it came to their baptismal service we parted company from them. Other Assemblies had visits from us from time to time. If became fun on Sundays, 'Where will we go to-day?'

Preaching appointments were sparse and Robert had the awful humiliation of ministers refusing to have him in their pulpit. They assumed that because he was a politician he couldn't simply preach the Gospel of Jesus Christ. Robert felt deeply hurt by this but he would say very little.

The pulpit, to Robert, was a sacred place, reserved for proclamation of the Gospel. Never in all his time in Suffolk did he use it as a platform for politics, in fact the opposite was true. Whenever he was asked to speak at a political rally he would always find a place to speak of his Saviour. He regarded South Belfast as his parish and his seventy-five thousand constituents as parishioners and treated them as such, whatever their political or religious persuasion, taking endless time in his advice centres to listen to peoples' problems.

In these last days before our Lord's return Robert felt he couldn't miss an opportunity. We began fasting one day a week at this point, a habit we kept up for many years. Robert was invited to speak at one of the sessions at a week-end conference in Corrymeela, Ballycastle. The conference had invited speakers from all political persuasions including some Republic of Ireland government officials. When we arrived the only other politician in sight was Peter McLachlan. The debate got under way with the theme 'Ulster Politics and Christian Morality.' Robert spoke:

> *'The problems of Northern Ireland are the result of three things . . . the Roman Catholic Church, International Marxism and ecumenical confusion. As a British Israelite I believe that scripture can be interpreted and understood very clearly in the light of current events.'*

He elaborated and went on to say, 'If the UK is to survive, then violent elements whose purpose is to destroy must be dealt with, and if that involves killing, then that has got to be.'

The debate began in earnest with the thirty or so people present attacking Robert from all sides. There was a pause and a man opposite spoke,

'I think we are doing Mr Bradford an injustice.'

At last, one level-headed person here I thought. I relaxed a little, but 'We are treating him as a rational sane person, and he is obviously nothing of the sort.'

And so it went on hot and heavy, with Robert answering all they threw at him. He tried to lighten the atmosphere.

'I'm beginning to feel like a mangy old lion being thrown

to the Christians.' There was some laughter but it didn't have the desired effect.

No matter where we looked we did not succeed in buying a house. Then came the bright idea of buying a plot of land and building on it with the thought that this would be cheaper, but plots weren't easy to come by. We discovered that a friend or ours owned some land at New Forge Lane, in South Belfast. We borrowed from the bank and bought it.

'Even if we can't keep up the payments,' Robert said, 'we can always sell it at a profit.'

The salary that had seemed so enormous to us at first was obviously not meant to be a sole stipend. Most of the other MP's had a job besides, but as Robert rarely took payment for taking services that meant my salary was really needed. Living in London was a very expensive business for Robert. Taking constituents who visited him for a meal or coffee all added up. I advised a cut-back but Robert's attitude was that it was the experience of a lifetime for each one and not to be denied. It thrilled him to treat people.

I was at work in the operating theatre one day, scrubbed in the middle of a case when I looked up to see Sister Connelly looking at me. It was a strange pitying look. I knew instantly it was about Robert. Something had happened! Was he shot?

'No, no,' she said, 'he took ill on the plane coming home from London, he has been taken to the City Hospital. It's a pain in his leg.'

She knew by my face I had instantly thought of deep venous thrombosis.

'It mightn't be, he's conscious. There's someone scrubbing to take over from you, try to carry on for a few minutes.'

My mask was soggy with my tears, and I couldn't see to hand the oblivious surgeon the instrument he required. I tried to cope looking sideways, knowing I could contaminate the whole tray if my tears fell on it or I breathed through this sodden mask onto the open wound. It seemed an age before the other girl took over.

I don't remember the short drive to the other hospital, just the look of Robert's grey ashen face as I came round the curtain in Casualty. He was lying on a trolley looking very ill indeed. His colleague John Carson was with him, the MP for North Belfast.

'He wanted to go home but I insisted he came here,' he said.

I was so grateful, his blood pressure was barely readable.

Through my mind flashed all the possibilities if this clot broke up. A heart attack, a stroke, . . . my mind whirled. Finally he was transferred to a medical ward under a Dr Connon. I had gone home to bring up pyjamas and other necessities and I missed Dr Connon but the ward Sister called me in late in the evening.

'We have done a lung scan and your husband has multible emboli. I don't need to tell you that the next twenty-four to forty-eight hours are critical.'

The heparinised drip was in place and I sat down beside Robert again and tried to laugh and joke with him for the rest of the time until I had to leave.

By now he was bright enough to chat and he told me what had happened. He had woken in his rather crummy bed-sit close to Westminster. 'I woke up with a leg cramp in time for the early flight and I bashed the leg around to relieve the spasm.'

Thus giving yourself multiple emboli,' I thought.

'I wouldn't go away so I got dressed and hobbled to the plane. I started to feel ill as we passed over Liverpool because the last thing I remember was the pilot speaking which was normally about there. I tried to tap the others in front on the shoulder but I was too weak. I thought I was dying so I prayed, "I'm already thirty thousand feet up Lord, couldn't you just take me all the way and end this awful feeling?" I came to as we landed and tried to persuade them not to make a fuss. They let everyone else off, then dealt with me.'

I didn't tell him that if he's gone home to bed as he had wanted he probably would have died on me.

Visiting hour was nearly over and the gawking eyes of the other visitors were really too much for him to bear. They seemed to expect him to sit up and wave to them all. Instead he ended up with the bed clothes almost over his face to escape their stares.

I put in a terrible night in the flat. I phoned to say I wouldn't be in to work until later, so about ten a.m. I arrived in the ward to find Robert prepared for a gastroscopy. I felt so sorry for him as I frequently assisted with them and knew it wasn't pleasant. He was quite cheerful. Sister had taken pity on him and moved him into a sideward and I got a chance to talk to Dr Connon.

'I feel he's almost out of danger now,' he continued his diagnosis. 'The 'flu bug Robert had about a fortnight ago may, I think, have caused a roughening of the vein in his leg, causing a clot to form, hence his condition.'

I was very relieved.

'If I'm right, he will have no further trouble. We are doing a gastroscopy this morning to make sure he isn't going to bleed from the old ulcer site. Then we'll get him on to warfarin and he can go home.'

I stayed most of the day and then eased back to work the next day, mainly because I needed to be occupied.

Robert wasn't an easy patient and I felt sorry for the nurses. Late one evening I was about to leave when the night Superintendent doing her rounds came in. She started to fuss that the high window above Robert's head was open. Robert leapt up, heparin drip and all, stood on his pillows and pushed it closed. I thought the poor woman was going to have apoplexy! And that wasn't the worst. A heparin infusion or drip, has to be carefully regulated or it will cause internal bleeding and the nurses would be in frequently to check it. Robert would mischievously turn it on full and then regulate it again.

'Just flushing the system,' he would chuckle.

'It's dangerous, don't muck about with it.' I knew he was doing it mostly for my benefit.

'After you left that first evening, I had a visit from the hospital chaplain. He asked what had happened so I told him, do you know what he said?'

"Oh, that's terribly dangerous, clots can break off and land anywhere, you could end up a vegetable or have a coronary."

Some Job's comforter he was. I had been so ill I hadn't thought of the consequences, but I did then!' Robert kept asking for Towser and Boo. I really had to lock them in a lot with work and the hospital visits. I decided that I would smuggle Towser in. Not a very hygienic idea but I thought it would help Robert get in another endless day. I tucked

Towser into my anorak and had him out again before anyone knew. Robert just adored that pup. The next day he was allowed home.

I arranged to take some holidays that were due and we decided to go to Dublin for a few days. We didn't inform anyone, feeling that we were safe enough if no-one knew. Robert stayed on for the rest of the week when I had to return to work. The next day Parliament made the decision to stay in the Common Market. Robert was distracted. He had somehow hoped we wouldn't take that step. He entered an Anglican church to meditate and read the open prayer book at the reading for that day:

Therefore hear the word of the Lord, you scornful men,
Who rule this people who are in Jerusalem,
Because you have said, 'We have made a covenant with death,
And with Sheol we are in agreement.
When the overflowing scourge passes through,
It will not come to us,
For we have made lies our refuge,
And under falsehood we have hidden ourselves.'
Therefore thus says the Lord God:
'Behold I lay in Zion a stone for foundation,
A tried stone, a precious corner-stone, a sure foundation;
Whoever believes will not act hastily.
Also I will make justice the measuring line,
And righteousness the plummet;
The hail will sweep away the refuge of lies,
And the waters will overflow the hiding place.
Your covenant with death will be annulled,
And your agreement with Sheol will not stand;
When the overflowing scourge passes through,
Then you will be trampled down by it.
As often as it goes out it will take you;
For morning by morning it will pass over,
And by day and by night;
It will be a terror just to understand the report.'
For the bed is too short for a man to stretch out on,
And the covering so narrow that he cannot wrap himself in it.
                                        (Isaiah 28. 14–20 RAV.)

He phoned me from Dublin to tell me what his God has said.

Robert was finding London interesting but lonely. He phoned me every night to talk over the day's events. Bill Craig and he would escape from Westminster and go and have a meal together if the pressure of ridiculous speeches got too much. I was very grateful to Bill Craig in those days for one special reason, he was expanding Robert's culinary tastes. Robert basically liked plain food and I liked adding interesting sauces to liven up the diet. Under Bill Craig's guidance Robert acquired a taste for many interesting foods, even Stilton cheese, all of which made cooking more fun for me.

Robert's advice centres had been going a year now and although police advice was that he shouldn't have a set routine, Robert knew how difficult it was for pensioners to travel from one area to another, even if they had the bus fare to spare.

I saved up all my holidays from work and we planned a four-week trip to Mississippi for Robert to take four separate week Missions. We were to leave on Friday evening. How exciting it would be. Robert had told me so much about the lovely people he had met that I couldn't wait to get there.

Ben Gerald met us at the airport in Jackson, Mississippi in the early hours of the morning and took us to his home. I liked him and his wife and family instantly. They weren't the gushy noisy Americans I had met as tourists, but a gentle quiet family that made us feel instantly at home.

In the morning Robert was to preach for Ben and I found out what jet lag was. I tried to focus on Robert in the pulpit but whatever way I winked or scringed I could see four of him. I spent the service wondering which was the real one.

Ben took us to Vicksburg, Mississippi immediately after church for 'dinner on the ground' at the church where we were to spend our first week's Mission, or 'Revival', as the Americans called it. Each family had brought a dish of food and the church hall was packed with the congregation eating from paper plates on their knees. The food was so extraordinarily different that I had to try a little piece of everything. The lovely way they had of mixing sweet and savoury salads together was an entirely new experience for me. A gospel group that had played at the morning service stayed and played on and off all afternoon. It was a delight to get to know these American Christians, then pop into the church, spend half an hour listening to the gospel in song, then wander out and talk to some more people. The whole day was given to the church and everyone was enjoying it so much.

'This is how it should be,' I thought, 'being a Christian is such fun, if only our people in Ulster could recapture this joy, life would be so much easier.'

'Let me introduce you both to Mr and Mrs Bruce.' It was their minister Rev Brand Jenkins introducing us to the people we were to stay with. Mr Bruce was very tall and quiet with an American crew-cut. Mrs Bruce had a lovely smile and warm hands.

'How will I keep Robert in line for a whole week for these quiet retired folk?' I thought frantically.

The evening service was a happy time for all, with contributions from the group and the choir and I had my first taste of their praise services. With piano and organ both playing, a chorus leader conducted from the pulpit and kept congregation, piano and organ together, the result of which raised the roof. Robert preached better than I had ever heard him and despite his accent the people seemed to have no trouble understanding him. This congregation paid for time on the local radio to broadcast their services, this was one of their ways of evangelising Vicksburg.

Our cases were transferred to the Bruce's beautifil Oldsmobile and we were whisked off to their home. As we drove slowly down their gravel driveway we saw a rustic-brick bungalow set amongst high trees, a really peaceful setting. Behind the bungalow the land sloped down to a lake. A crazy paving path and steps led through the towering trees to a small private jetty. It was like a piece of heaven on earth. We weren't in the house two minutes until Robert had his shoes off and his feet on the hearth.

'Thank goodness he doesn't have smelly feet.' I thought. 'Will you behave?' I pleased, 'we have to stay here a week.'

'They won't mind,' he grinned mischieviously.

I despaired. In a very short time we got to know Florence and Webb Bruce and found in them a well of fun that matched our own. We had a beautiful week in their home and a week of blessing in the church. Brand set a spanking pace for Robert, with early morning TV chat shows, lunch at the Civitan Club etc, and our feet hardly touched the ground. The week came to an end very quickly and there were many tears shed when we had to part.

Our second mission was in West Monroe, Louisiana. It was to be a totally different experience. Robert had met Rev Johnny Hankin, the young minister, on his previous visit and he came to drive us to Louisiana on the Friday night after the service. He explained that they had wanted us to stay with them in their trailer but a couple who always put up the visiting preacher, had seemed offended at the suggestion.

'They are very difficult to wake,' Johnny added hesitantly as we stood ringing the doorbell after our long journey into the early hours of the morning. Fifteen minutes later when we had created a racket fit to waken the dead, a sleepy woman's head, bedecked in curlers, peered around the door. Johnny Hankin had made a comment that she never stopped talking and within twenty minutes we knew what he meant – she hadn't drawn breath! Her husband Jimmy didn't appear until breakfast time. Very tired and very over-fed we would have dearly loved to skip breakfast but we couldn't offend our new hosts.

We listened to Boyce in amazement: obviously a dear soul, she was so strung up she couldn't stop. When we replied to her, we found she continued right on in a tone lower, then raised her voice as soon as she thought you ought to have finished. Jimmy was a lovely big man who would intercede for us on occasions when he thought it was overpowering with a 'shut up, Boyce'. This meant she lowered her tone down two levels but went right on going.

One of the biggest problems here was laundry. In America the clothes are manufactured to be crease-free and the fact that I needed to iron Robert's clerical shirts each time they were washed caused a problem. An iron was eventually produced from some long-forgotten corner and I thought,

'That's us down in their estimation to "pigs in the kitchen" again.'

The week in West Monroe was so totally different from Vicksburg. The church was equally beautiful in a different way. The people in both places were so hospitable for it to be a problem. We were given a hearty breakfast by Boyce of American biscuits or scones, scrambled eggs, bacon and coffee and then we would be in someone's house for lunch and somewhere else for an evening meal and then supper after church. By the end of the second week we both felt ill. It was so hard to say 'No' to such lavish hospitality. As in Vicksburg, each housewife only had one chance to entertain us and so each produced mountainous quantities of lovely food. Johnny and Bonnie Hankins understood, having been on Revival themselves, and helped us cut out some meals.

We met lovely people everywhere we went. One gentleman took some photos of us and at the end of the week his wife presented us with portraits she had done of us.

'My talent is God-given: God healed me from a serious illness and I promised to use my talent to his glory,' she told us.

Johnny Hankins took us to an American football game but it was all of half-time before we had the vaguest idea what was happening. I was most impressed at the family atmosphere in the terraces. At any soccer games I had been to at home with Robert the language of the spectators left a lot to be desired, but here even the tiniest children present were not likely to be offended by the behaviour of the adults or teenagers around. One lovely girl called Nancy discovered we liked 'Kentucky Fried Chicken' and when it was her turn to entertain us she produced buckets-full. She then presented us with Helen Steiner Rice's book *Just For You*, a beautiful book of poems.

We survived that week with Boyce and Jimmy and got very fond of them. The third week was to be spent in Monticello, a small country town. Both Vicksburg and West Monroe had been large cities and this would be an interesting contrast. This week we were to stay in a motel and a very different time was organised by the Minister, Rev Dr Sellers, with Robert talking to students in a local University in the mornings and less enormous eating out sessions. A small community centred around a crossroads, so Monticello wasn't hard to get to know.

The beautiful new Sanctuary had been opened that Sunday morning and we went straight into the revival. A very tragic story emerged out of that small community. A young couple had lost both their children in a middle of the night fire at their home. What should have been two miserable people, turned out to be two shining rays of sunshine for the Lord. Their testimony of how God had brought them through their tragedy was awe-inspiring. Their attitude was that God had allowed them to have two precious children for a short time and they were grateful, some others had never even had that.

During that week large welts developed on my arms and legs and we finally realised they were some sort of mosquito bite that I was allergic to. The Southern Americans say they grow everything bigger – in this case I was inclined to agree with them!

Preaching in the Mississippi heat was taking its toll on Robert and he was finding it hard-going, though very enjoyable. The relaxation of the motel room was a very pleasantly quiet end to the days.

Our last week was to be spent in Alabama, in a little town called Thomasville. It was really 'out in the sticks,' we were informed, and this was not a joke as we discovered when we traversed the dirt roads. Dr Sellers hinted on the way down,

'They get up rather early down here,' he cautioned, 'and they're inclined to expect you to do the same, at least that's how it was last Revival I did for them.'

'They surely won't to-morrow,' I thought, being Saturday, as we didn't expect to get there till the small hours of the morning.

A small wooden bungalow was the manse and Rev and Mrs Travis Crawford greeted us and showed us straight to our room.

'Those pretty net curtains aren't going to keep much of the early morning sun out.' I thought.

We feel asleep quickly, despite the coyotes howling in the forest and what seemed like almost immediately the door practically fell off its hinges with the hammering of a fist.

'Breakfast,' Travis yelled.

Robert sat bolt upright in bed in shock, opened his mouth to reply none too politely so I stuffed a pillow in his face and sat on him. I released him when our host's footsteps had faded away.

'They're not serious,' he said exasperated.

We looked at our watches, it was 5.45 am, and the sun

had barely risen.

'Sellers sure wasn't joking!' I added in my best southern American droll to make him laugh. I pulled on a housecoat I had found behind the door.

'I'll go to-day and you lie on, and you can go to-morrow.'

I tried to be as cheerful as my hosts, even though my head wouldn't stay up straight without the help of an arm to lean on. About half way through breakfast Robert arrived fully dressed, politeness having overcome his irritation. By half-past eight that evening our hosts were yawning and preparing for bed and we were as bright as buttons. We went to our room and read for hours, then foudnd it difficult to sleep. We came to a decision that we couldn't stick a week of this so at breakfast next morning Robert proposed to our hosts that we would skip breakfast as we didn't normally eat any at home – which was quite true – and get up in time for their morning coffee about nine am. It proved an excellent arrangement, as did staying up talking or watching TV when they had retired to bed.

Preaching in the church Robert found rather difficult – and not just because of the poor air conditioning system: there seemed to be a hardened atmosphere and Robert would come out of the pulpit looking grey and weak with sweat pouring off his brow. I really wondered whether he would collapse.

'I just can't break through this barrier,' he said in desperation. 'The people all seem to be lovely but somehow I'm banging my head against a brick wall.'

Robert preached until he was weak and I prayed with seeming no avail. On the last night the whole congregation lined up to shake hands and many tears were shed at our parting.

As we came home for yet another Christmas to get through in our childless home, our God had planned a glorious surprise. There was a little girl for us to adopt. The unspeakable joy that that gave us is impossible to put into words. Such fun we had shopping for this treasure and then smuggling a cot and other essentials into the flat without the neighbours seeing.

Christmas that year was a magical time for us. Claire was everything we had hoped and prayed for. The nativity scene came alive for us as we bent over the sleeping form in the cot

116

in the junk room we had hastily cleared and decorated.

Our lives now revolved around this precious newcomer. But all was not easy. Getting Claire to sleep was an impossible task. She didn't yet trust us and had to have us in sight, which meant long hours sitting cramped on the floor of her bedroom with her determination to watch with at least one eye. If you tried to creep out after a weary hour she would bounce up and it was back to square one. Robert was back to Parliament again and I was left to cope. Our lives had done a complete turn around in two years. From working full-time and being out every evening at church meetings and very busy all the time I was now on my own for most of the week, totally confined in the evenings, and apart from lots more washing and ironing I had little to occupy my mind. Life became extremely difficult for me. Robert had his time in London where he was constantly under pressure in Parliament, and when at home he had his Saturday and Monday advice centres to attend, he would come home wanting to enjoy his little daughter and found it difficult to understand why I was finding life impossible.

I tried to explain that it was just everything. The church people for the most part I had to avoid in case it be thought I was interfering in the church business, and then there were the dogs in the area.

Robert had been with me when Towser had been attacked by the next door corgi. Robert kicked the corgi away and got bitten for his touble. That minor *fracas* developed into a real problem. The dogs couldn't go out with me to the shops without being attacked and it got that Boo was so scared when I let them out onto the grass that she would run straight back upstairs with unfortunate consequences.

It all accelerated to the point where I couldn't take Claire out in the pram without carrying a stick with me. Life seemed to close in around me with a mountain of tension.

Robert had kept very quiet on the subject of Garden Parties at Buckingham Palace and it was a couple of years before I discovered we could put our names in a hat in the hope of being picked to go. When I discovered it his face looked tragic. You could see the '£' signs spinning up before his eyes like a vending machine as the thought of me shopping for an outfit for a Palace Garden Party. Add to that the fact that he hated to dress up for anything. Weddings were a case in point. We were always the last to arrive and the first to leave, sometimes even before the bridge and groom.

'I have to make some important phone calls,' I was told as I was dragged out of yet another reception. Finally in 1977 an invitation arrived . . .

The Lord Chamberlain is
commanded by Her Majesty to invite
The Reverend Robert Bradford and Mrs Bradford to an
Afternoon Party in the Garden of Buckingham Palace.

We had set off to the airport when it occured to me that the invitation was still on the mantelpiece and so was our pass to the Palace. We had to turn round and go back and get the next Shuttle. Then it was a mad rush to get ready in the Family Room at the House of Commons with others trying to do the same.

Finally we arrived at the appropriate gate and I was dragged up the long gravel path at a fierce lick. Glowing profusely I was whisked past the beautiful lake with its stately pink flamingoes onto the lawn where people were crowded in three channels preparing to greet their Royal hosts.

'I've arranged for us to be introduced to the Queen.' Robert charged on determined to get through. I gulped and held on tightly to his hand, saying, 'Excuse me, excuse me,' as we pushed into the centre. The gentleman in charge of the introductions spotted Robert and pulled us through the ranks placing us in a position where we could be introduced.

It was incredible to be so close to Her Majesty Queen Elizabeth. As she approached, talking graciously to those she met, she would walk first to one side and then the other to speak to people who weren't being formally introduced, knowing it was the experience of a lifetime for so many.

She was approaching us. My knees were knocking. I went really cold. Would I remember to call her Ma'am? What on earth would I say to her? Suddenly she was standing in front of us smiling. I managed a wobbly curtsey. She chatted lightly and Robert did most of the replying. Knowing she must speak first, he finally got the opening he was looking for to put in,

'Your loyal people in Ulster are looking forward so much to your impending Jubilee visit to your Province and pray that you will come and go in safety.'

She was obviously pleased and as she took her leave of us I thought with relief that I had survived remarkably well. Robert grabbed my hand and took off again.

'Calm down, surely we can relax now,' I said.

'Don't you want to meet the Duke of Edinburgh?' his eyes twinkled as he rushed on.

Into this other row we pushed and again we were spotted and placed in a position. I survived yet another curtsey without falling over as my stiletto heels sank into the grass.

We made our way to the tea-tent and helped ourselves to buffet-style goodies and a cup of tea. We sank into two vacant seats and I sighed with relief. We reminisced over the last chaotic half hour and the thrill of it all. We didn't know till much later that a couple from Northern Ireland had seen us presented to the Queen, then turned to the other channel just in time to see, with total amazement, us introduced to the Duke of Edinburgh. Robert's way of never doing things by halves still took me by surprise occasionally.

The Queen's visit to Ulster was about to begin when an invitation to a Reception at Hillsborough Castle in her honour, came through the door. A new outfit was definitely in order in case the Queen recognised my last one. Robert feigned despair but quietly enjoyed my excitement.

I was a lovely sunny day again as we wandered over the lawn. Robert had been asked if we wanted to be introduced but we decided it would be unfair as there were only a limited number who could meet the Queen and we had had our chance. We were standing in the crowd as Her Majesty walked by. She spotted Robert and came over.

'Haven't I met you before?' she smiled at him.

He bowed as the group parted for him.

'We were introduced at your Garden Party last month, my name is Bradford.'

'Ah yes,' she said, 'I remember,' and they chatted for a few moments further. Robert couldn't get over the fact that she had remembered him.

'She must be introduced to hundreds of people every week, imagine her remembering my face!'

'Once seen never forgotten,' I teased.

Robert threw himself one hundred per cent into the fight against pornography and his fight to get peace in our beloved province involved trying to get at the roots of the terrorist IRA. He began to collect a lot of information about their fund-raising activities and investigate possible links with the Royal Victoria Hospital, and as this was reported in the press there began a campaign of sending parcels to our home. There were pink suits ordered for Robert, bullworks sent, books, insurance men, anything that was thought would cause us annoyance. For the most part we found it hilarious and couldn't wait to see what we had been sent next. The annoyance was in humping large parcels to the Post Office to return them. It seemed to be mainly a one person campaign as we discovered from the address which always began 'Wine Lodge'. Being strictly brought up as teetotallers that was hardly a name we would use for our home.

We began to think seriously about building on our plot of land and I threw myself into deciding what I wanted our home to be like. It was lovely to start from scratch and plan it just as we wanted it. An architect's services were procured and we began in earnest. After what seemed interminable months the plans went out for tender and the building began. Claire was at playschool now and I was free for a few hours each morning. I treated myself regularly to a trip down to Botanic Avenue: I would buy a newspaper, sit in the corner of a quiet coffee shop and make a cup of coffee and a scone last an hour. This was my heaven. I needed so much to get away from the tensions in the Suffolk flat and those stolen hours became very precious to me.

Our new home took about twelve months to build and in the end we told the builder we were moving in in a month's time, ready or not. We had a very amicable relationship with the builder, who was easy to work with. So many people had told us they had gone through a terrible time with builders that I vowed I would not get angry. Work got done far better by a kind word than a cross one.

The move was great fun. We borrowed a large van and with the help of my brother and about four friends we shifted our furniture from the flat. Two rooms were finished in our new home and were lockable. We collected our extra boxes from their various storage points, in the Nicholson's spare room, my brother's garage, my mother's attic and garage. The two rooms were piled high. Robert had to preach the next day so his clerical gear had to be located and taken care of. We spent the next few weeks living with my mother in Donaghadee, but as far as the builder knew we were actually in the house. I had made the curtains in the flat and 'wee Jimmy' put up the curtain rails so that we could have some privacy. As yet the kitchen wasn't installed and the plumber rigged up a stand pipe for me, slops were disposed of down the loo. The front garden had to be built up and a path laid but for now we had a couple of planks across the mud and a gang plank over a four foot drop at the front door. It had been terrifying watching Robert and the others try to take the piano up the plank when we moved in, they got stuck half way and the piano swayed on its borrowed trolley as they frantically grabbed it. It survived and though slightly out of tune was none the worse. It was within the first few days that my neighbour Eileen came to introduce herself with the house-warming present of a lovely fruit cake. I couldn't have been more thrilled. To be out of that terrible flat with its outlook on to the corrugated iron gates of the peace line, to find that I had again nice neighbours. Our neighbours in Suffolk had been really helpful. On one occasion when the fan belt had gone in the car, 'wee Jimmy' had come up to fix it when Robert was in London and I was out. Several of them had come to tackle him to see who he was and why he was touching our car.

Getting everything finished in the house was a long slow process. On one occasion when the builder decided a payment was due he spent the day sitting in the garage sipping cups of tea. Robert came in and out past him refusing to be worn down as he felt the work that was supposed to be done wasn't completed. By evening Robert said, 'I'll have to pay him, I can't look at that expression any longer.' The drive-way was one of the last things to get done. Finally the scree was laid and the edging stones set in concrete and the tar-macadam was to come the next day. Our oil-fired central heating was not completely wired up to the timer but could

121

be turned on manually. I stepped down into the garage one morning to press the button to find myself up to my ankles in icy water. I screamed with shock. Robert appeared rather bleary eyed. The top of the driveway was too low and the whole of New Forge Lane was draining, after the torrential rain, down into our garage. Our architect hastily devised a series of drains to combat the problem and a trough at the garage threshold to catch any overflow.

The tension eased considerably for me now that we had our own home and I concentrated on decorating it. Claire and the dogs were beside themselves with joy at all the space and the peace was so lovely. The split-level house was of rather moderate proportions but adequate for our needs. It had a big lounge with a large picture window to the road facing east which got the morning sun and one to the back with a view of Divis mountain which took in some glorious sunsets. The kitchen and dining-room had the same lovely view. The bathroom and spare bedroom were beside the front door and the other bedrooms were downstairs, plus a long narrow basement Robert intended to use as an office. Up until now he had used the Jordan's home but he felt it was an unfair arrangement for the rest of the Jordan household.

Robert purchased a desk and went out and chose carpet tiles. His enthusiasm knew no bounds. Not known for his manual work he set to and laid the tiles himself. 'Wee Jimmy' just wouldn't believe it, in fact whenever it was mentioned, as it was often by Robert, Jimmy just looked sceptical and didn't comment.

We were justly proud of our new home. Robert could not find time to discuss the other various colour schemes and furnishings so I had to do it myself. It was no chore for me, I loved it! It was like a new lease of life.

'If you aren't gong to help' I commented, 'then I don't want any complaints that you don't like it when it's done.'

Robert agreed. His only stipulation being that he wanted lions on his gateposts.

It was very expensive trying to furnish and carpet this new home and we decided I would have to work again. Night duty seemed the only way of getting a reasonable wage and not letting Claire suffer. I applied for, and got a post as Staff Nurse in the Ulster Hospital working two nights, Wednesdays and Thursdays. When Robert was away, Jimmy and Sadie came and stayed overnight to help us out. While training to be a nurse I had loathed night-duty and hoped never to have to do it again, but this was necessity.

We had a lot of entertaining to do to make up for the three years in the flat. Sundays were now fairly hectic with Robert having lots of preaching appointments. It had taken all this time to build up to services every Sunday, but now that he was really in demand again, he loved it. 'It's such a release to preach, I can cope with all the strain of Westminster when I can preach at the week-ends.'

Mondays and Tuesdays I fed my freezer for the next week-end's entertaining, then Friday and Saturday nights we entertained friends and political colleagues.

Our life together now was totally different from the way it had started off in the manse. We had Claire to consider in everything we did. Robert's advice centres were a big security worry. Where some other politicians locked themselves behind doors, Robert felt he had to be out and amongst the people to be effective. We developed a Saturday routine of going out in the car together after his advice centre was finished and the fifth Saturdays in the month were sent from heaven occasionally to lighten the load. We took a picnic and ended up in the craziest places. We were found on one occasion by a farmer, with the car parked in the middle of his field which he had come to plough up. We went anywhere we would meet no-one, the dogs could run about and Claire could use up some of her excess energy. Robert and I relaxed with our sandwiches and coffee or on colder days Irish stew, while the rest of the family ran free. It was a chance to chat, to joke together. To get time together as the awful pressure we lived under threatened to keep us apart.

The police were calling at our door with ominous regularity now.

'There's a threat to hit your East Belfast Advice Centre this week, we'll double the guard.'

Or perhaps it was just a general threat to be watchful. The routine of checking under the car everytime I used it was a useless idea I felt as I didn't know what I was looking for. If there was a lump on the underside I sure wouldn't know whether it belonged there or not.

Robert's life in Westminster was really getting him down. 'Week after week I sit there and work on speeches for the House. Then I sit in the Chamber and wait my turn and try to point out again how many innocent people are being slaughtered in Ulster. I try to get through to those Englishmen that "enough is enough" but they don't or won't see it. They cannot grasp the fact that the terrorists aren't interested in anyone's democratic rights or principles. They want to bomb, mutilate and kill people until we surrender our beloved province into their hands. They don't understand that we *won't* surrender. No more will I stop working against the terrorists because they threaten me. Though my biggest fear is that if they did anything to you or Claire or even the dogs, I would not be able to control my rage.'

And so life became more and more intense for us. The constant pressure of being elected to the seat of power but being helpless to actually change things drastically really began to affect Robert. Home at week-ends things were no better. There was yet another police or UDR funeral to attend and yet another widow and children to visit and comfort. The toll of lives mounted on.

Each year Robert headed off to Mississippi in the South to take 'Revivals'. He was paid out of the collections and this helped pay his fare and enabled us to still afford a family holiday together. This was his only contact with the church there and it became very important to him. We tried to help them in our way, by paying the fare for one of their teenagers to come over for a visit. Robert organised employment for them and they paid us back while still being able to have a holiday and see Ulster. While we were still in the flat in Suffolk, Valeda had come on such a visit and worked in an office in London. We had hoped to get her accommodation in a flat there but it fell through at the last minute and we had to rent a house for those weeks and go and live there.

Next year it was Rev Ben Gerald's son Bernie's turn. Bernie was about eighteen years old and very quiet – I thought! I was to discover otherwise. He arrived one Friday night sooner than expected on his stand-by ticket and we had already arranged a dinner party. Bernie decided to join us rather than give in to his jet-lag. The meal was in full swing with Robert keeping the conversation lively by interspersing his latest jokes. Bernie was sitting beside him looking rather wane and tired. I served the steaks and everyone helped themselves to vegetables when I noticed Bernie heaping mustard onto his first bite. I tried to signal to him across the table without interrupting everyone's chat and he signalled back that it was alright, he liked mustard. He had it spread a quarter-inch thick all over. I watched desparingly as he put it in his mouth and then watched him go redder and redder. I ran for a large glass of water and as the whole table realised what the drama was about we all dissolved into laughter. There's a vast difference between English and American mustard! 'Poor Bernie, what an introduction to Ulster,' I thought.

Earlier that day he had been interrogated by the police at the airport in London and finally had the sense to say he was coming to stay with us. 'Why didn't you say that in the first place?' the policeman retorted sending him on his way. Bernie was great fun. His droll sense of humour often had us in stitches as he described the antics of the men he worked with. His way of combating their bad language was to break into a loud chorus of 'Dixie'.

It was lovely having him around the house when Robert had to go away. The weary plod up to the airport and down twice a week could be very monotonous. As far as Claire was concerned it was her Daddy's airport and he owned all the planes too. Her logic was that he spent most of his life there so it must be his.

We had graduated to a Ford Granada car which I had taken delivery of when Robert was ill in bed with flu. I had a horrific journey home from choosing it, convinced that it would be scratched before he saw it. There was some fear in his look when I arrived home and told him I had chosen a pink one. He struggled out of bed and came to the window to look. It was an interesting colour but hardly pink. A light metallic red was perhaps a better description with a black vinyl roof. We had had three dark green cars in a row and this was a lovely change. Robert had been criticised on several occasions for not supporting home industry by owning a foreign car. Now that was rectified. It was a car we both became very fond of.

The garden was taking shape and flower-beds were dug

and stocked, mostly from my mother's prolific garden. I went in search of some trees. I wanted a cherry tree for the front garden near the rose bed. At the local garden centre I found a few cherry trees that were being sold cheap because they had lost their labels. I didn't mind what sort of cherry I had so I bought one and Robert helped me plant it near the front door. It began to bloom a few months later with tiny pale pinky white flowers.

'I'm afraid we've disrupted it, I hope we don't lose it,' I commented.

It turned out to be what we called our 'silly tree.' It bloomed twice or three times a year. Our 'silly tree' was interesting to watch as we never knew quite when it was going to bloom again.

It took quite a few years for me to discover all the perks of Robert's job. The nicest were the multiple free warrants for trips to London each year. Only one year did I manage to fit in all the trips I was allowed. It was exciting to visit that metropolis and be able to shop for household items, to go through Hamleys with Claire and watch her eyes get larger and larger at the fabulous array of toys. Our next stop was always Harrods for lunch-time, not specifically to eat but to visit the pet department when all the puppies and kittens were awake and being fed.

I arranged to meet Robert on one of these visits and have a snack lunch in Harrods' snack-bar beside the boutique for younger people. Claire wasn't with me on this spree. I waited and waited; then I remembered there was a Health Food snack-bar on the ground floor and wondered if Robert had mistakenly gone there, so I got the lift down and fortunately Robert was just about to enter it.

'Do you realize "dear",' he said sarcastically, 'there are at least six snack-bars in this building and I have been round five of them?'

'We could have spent the rest of our lives wandering from floor to floor and never met up!' he said.

'Just think of all the lovely men I'd have met, though,' I said, and his fury was short-lived. To make up for our hasty lunch, that evening Robert took me to a small Italian restaurant he had found. It was dimly lit and we were served with extraordinary food. I hadn't the vaguest idea what I was eating but it was delicious. The waiters were very friendly extrovert Italians who frequently broke into song and you might have half an aria from them over one course as they served the tables.

The next day it was back home, but with a few more thrilling memories to think on in the dull lonely days that lay ahead.

6

Robert's visits to the Southern States of America were now combined with trips to Washington DC to get to know some American politicians. He was always on the look out for opportunities to put the Protestant point of view, to share what was really happening in Ulster in this terrorist war and if possible to encourage industrial investment in our part of Britain.

On this trip to the USA Claire and I were joining Robert along with Ruth who was to sing at the revivals. It was lovely for me to have some adult female company.

On a previous trip Robert had passed out on a plane and ended up in a hospital in Atlanta, so this trip I was watching him like a hawk for any signs of illness. Doctors had been unable to find a solution except that they thought altitude was a contributory factor. Claire and Ruth were asleep when it happened. Robert squeezed my hand and I was instantly alert. He looked at me from his ashen face but his speech was too slurred for me to understand. His pulse was very slow and weak, almost impossible to find. I jumped across the two prone figures, standing on the arm rests and ran to find the stewardess.

'I need some brandy quickly, my husband's ill.'

She fumbled through the drawers taking an age.

'I'll pay you later,' I called as I ran.

Robert was almost unconscious. I dragged him upright from where he had slumped across my seat and poured a small amount of brandy into the corner of his open mouth and he tried to swallow. I was terrifked that he was too far gone. I gave him some more and it dribbled out the side of his mouth, his eyes rolled upwards and he passed out. I felt for a pulse, I was sure he was gone. But under my fingers it came back and became stronger. Some of the brandy must have got there in time.

I hauled his legs on to the seat to get him as horizontal as possible and lifted Claire's sleeping form over the top to lie beside him so that he could stretch out over the three seats. His colour gradually returned and his condition improved. By the end of the flight he was weak but fine though I was in a shivery state of shock for quite a while. I didn't like to tell him how close I felt he had come. There was little point in seeing a doctor as he seemed fine. The problem was obviously on planes and now that I knew brandy helped I would keep some at hand.

Florence and Webb Bruce had planned a lovely surprise for us while Robert flew to Washington. They had booked us for two days into a hotel in Orlando, Florida to see Disney World and proceeded to drive Claire, Ruth and myself down there. It was an experience of a lifetime, though terribly hot, with temperatures in the nineties. Ruth and I queued for different rides for Claire and then decided to go to the Haunted House. With about twenty minutes to go before we got in, a thunderstorm hit us. Before we could move from the queue we were soaked through, but we decided that our light cotton dresses would dry quickly as soon as the sun came out. We were right – almost. We were into the house before we were completely dried out, so the cold air-conditioning seemed even colder and the ride more scary because of it.

We had a fabulous time with our beautiful generous friends. The journey back to Mississippi was long but we stopped frequently for cups of coffee, meals and to stretch our legs. Robert was back from Washington when we returned. Ruth sang on the Sunday in the Vicksburg church and I had my first introduction to some of Evie Torquist's gospel songs. The next two weeks in Monroe and Marion, Lousiana were electric with Robert commenting on his feeling that, after Ruth had sung, such was the message that there was little need for him to preach. The atmosphere was really set.

His sermons were long but he held his congregation spell-bound. He would rest them gently now and then with an appropriate story taken from some of F W Boreham's books, Francis Gray's *Friendship* books or drawn from his own childhood experiences. You could have heard a pin drop. At the close Robert would make an appeal for people to come to the communion rail in full commitment of their lives to Jesus Christ. He would walk down from the pulpit and himself kneel in rededication. The Holy Spirit drew many people to the Lord in those weeks.

Claire was coping well with being up late every night at

church and my only problem was that she liked to mimic Robert. As he waved his arms in the pulpit she would copy and I would try to restrian her which only served to make her more determined. As Robert said a sentence she would say the last two words aloud after him, along with the appropriate arm gestures. Robert found it all highly amusing. It was hard to leave for home again, as we had made so many new friends in Monroe and Marion.

The plane trip home was uneventful. Robert avoided eating anything and kept his feet up on the wall in front of us for the whole trip. I had a miniature brandy in my pocket in case he should need it.

On occasions when Robert was stuck in London I took his advice centres. I began to understand why he liked to eat after them and not before. Listening for three or four hours to peoples' problem was very emotionally draining. One centre was in a 'fish-and-chippy' and it was difficult to conduct as other people could hear the conversation. Another was in a British Legion hall where an attempt was made to assassinate Robert. A girl had come inquiring if he would be coming and the caretaker had been suspicious about her manner and phoned the police. They gave chase to the two men who arrived with weapons but didn't manage to catch them. Police guards were made permanent for each building Robert was publicised to attend, but Robert was concerned about this as he felt it set the police up as an easy target and he knew they had many other duties they could be performing instead.

One Saturday I made my way to take one of those advice centres. The tiny room contained some eight chairs which made it very cramped. I positioned Claire in the corner with her colouring book and felt-tip pens and warned her to behave. The people came in with their various problems and I took notes to give to Robert. The door opened for the last person and a tramp walked in. Robert had warned me this might happen, but I hadn't warned Claire. The smell wasn't pleasant. He sat down, trying not to look directly at me.

Claire said, 'Mum,'
I said 'Shh!' knowing exactly what she thought by her face.
'But, Mum!'
'Shh!' I threatened.

130

'Oh but Mum!' By now she had curled her legs up in front of her and was holding her nose. Her eyes were out like organ stops.

'Be quiet!' I ordered. The poor man was shifting nervously on his seat, though there was no blush visible through the grime.

'Oh!' she said in exasperation and watched him over her knees.

I tried to listen to the poor man but kept wondering what on earth had happened to him to make him opt out of life so completely. I related this to Robert after he had heard Claire's version.

'I usually have him in complaining about the mice in his house and its conditions,' Robert said, 'then next I have the mice in complaining about him! There's no solution!'

I roared with laughter though underneath the fun I knew he cared very deeply.

I had many experiences of Robert's compassion for tramps and social outcasts. We could be happily walking along the street holding hands when he would excuse himself.

'I'll only be a minute.'

A tramp we had just passed in a doorway would be taken into a café and a meal set in front of him and we would be on our way again.

I picked Robert up one bitter winter's day after a Saturday advice centre and we headed off with our usual flask of hot Irish stew, sandwiches and coffee. Many National Trust parks were empty at this time of year and the dogs ran happily round the solitary car park while we ate and caught up on the week's events.

'I had a wee woman in today in a bad way.'

I turned to listen.

'I lent her some money.' He glanced sideways at me.

'Don't you think that might set a precedent?' I was a little scared.

'She reminded me so much of my Mum (Sadie). I just felt if she was ever in that position I would like to think someone would help her.'

There was no answer to that so I dropped the subject. Months later Robert commented one day,

'Do you know that little woman hasn't missed a month in

paying me back for that loan?'

Night duty had been taking its toll on me so as soon as we saw daylight financially, I quit. It was lovely to come out that zombie-like existence.

As Claire got older and spent a longer time in school, I looked for a part-time day job. Out of the blue came the chance of a post in a clinic about one mile from the house. I was given a week's refresher course, which I was very glad of, and was told to start on the ward in two days' time.

I had had a quiet day at home, having left Robert up at the airport for the early Shuttle flight to London. I collected Claire from school and went into the lounge to light the fire. I flicked on the TV

> *'The Rev Robert Bradford collapsed to-day on a plane to London, he was taken to the Cardiac Unit of a local London hospital.'*

The match burnt my fingers and I came out of my open mouthed daze. I sat for a minute to collect my thoughts, then I ran to lift the phone. I went through a string of emotions, ending in sheer anger. 'Why had none of his colleagues contacted me?' I knew there were some on his flight. I didn't know the bell on the phone was faulty and they had been trying all day. I was scared and furious. I picked up the phone to dial and a voice spoke. It was my sister-in-law. She said she would be straight over. I phoned Ulster Television.

'News-room please,' I tried to sound calm. 'Could you please tell me what hospital my husband is in?'

I tried to control my rage. They were dumbfounded that I didn't know.

'I'm only his wife!' I retorted very rudely, furious with everyone and very scared.

I phoned the hospital and it took an age to get through. If I had been out or away from the phone then I could have understood no-one being able to reach me but I had spent all day cleaning the house. The phone in the coronary care unit was answered and I coulnd't make head or tail of what the man was saying.

'Just a minute,' he said eventually.

Suddenly Robert's voice was on the line. Tears of relief rolled down my cheeks.

'I've been trying to get a message to you all day,' he said.

'I'm coming over,' I said.

'Don't be silly, I'm fine, please don't fuss.'

132

I'll get there about nine p.m. and . . . for once you are in no position to argue,' I retorted.

I put the phone down. The family rallied round and before very long they had Claire packed off to Donaghadee, I phoned the clinic to say I wouldn't be in the next, then I was off to catch a plane.

Robert looked up as I came in and grinned.

'You really made it,' he said.

Then he admitted that he would have been very disappointed if I hadn't come. He was wired to a heart monitor and *my* heart sank as I looked at his ECG tracing. It didn't look good. He seemed in fine form now, though his hair was annoying him.

'Will you wash it for me.?' he pleaded.

I told him it was impossible but he wouldn't take no for an answer. In the end I approached the charge nurse. He was a very pleasant black man who was fed-up to the teeth answering the phone to the press who wanted progress reports for their latest news programmes.

You're welcome to try to wash it, maybe it will settle him down.'

I thought he was being over-optimistic but took the end off the bed and proceeded to deck Robert in polythene. I had visions of electrocuting him or ruining the monitoring apparatus.

As I proceeded I asked, 'How on earth did you talk to me on the phone?'

'The charge nurse could't make you understand,' (his accent was difficult to interpret on the phone), 'so he pulled my bed over to the nurses' station and handed me the phone and said . . . "you talk to her!" '

I finished settling him down and then I left to find somewhere to stay.

In the morning I arrived to find they had had another crisis with him during the night when his pulse had dropped to about thirty. They hadn't been able to contact me. The doctor-in-charge had a chat with me. His diagnosis was that Robert was in a state of collapse from exhaustion.

'He's not sleeping and hasn't been for a number of years. He needs to relax. I have suggested to him that he will either have to go on to sleeping tablets or he could try a glass of port or sherry at bed-time. I feel that if his blood sample comes back clear, you can take him home to-day, so long as you "ground" him for a while.'

'That's easier said than done,' I thought.

'What about his heart? I didn't like the look of his ECG.' I said.

'I think that that is normal for Robert,' he replied.

A bell rang from the time of his previous collapse.

'I remembered Dr Connon saying he had a peculiar ECG, but I never actually saw the print-out.'

With that confirmation of his diagnosis the doctor said Robert could go home.

The plane journey home was a rather anxious time for us both but apart from Robert being weak the trip was uncomplicated. Robert admitted that he rarely slept when away from home which could mean up to four nights a week. We discussed the pro's and con's of sleeping tablets as opposed to 'booze'. We came down finally on the side of alcohol. It would only be at bed-time and as the years went by he could up the dose from wine to sherry or port, whereas to up the dose of drugs seemed more sinister. It was a toss-up between the very real dangers of alcohol or drugs. Not an easy decision.

The doctor's orders were a short break away, so Robert went to Majorca on his own for a week and then we booked a few days in Killarney for ourselves and our American friends Florence and Webb, who were arriving within a few days. The weather was glorious; the blue sky and radiant sea made for some lovely photos and a really relaxing time. We had thought it might have been a problem with the petrol strike in full swing in the Republic of Ireland but it was fairly easy to get a couple of gallons at a time. We let the tank get to the three-quarter mark and then topped it up again. Robert really relaxed and began to look more rested. Unfortunately, as we had expected, an election was called and we were back into the throes of it as soon as we returned to Belfast.

Robert's attitude had changed. Before his collapse he worked everyday until all his work was done to his satisfaction, no matter what the hour. From then on when he felt ill or became really exhausted he took time for himself, realising he was only capable of getting through so much in one lifetime. He took time each evening when home, while I prepared tea, to play with Claire in the garden and she became quite an adept footballer. He took time to push her on her swing and listen to her happy chatter.

This election he also took more gently, not because he cared any less but rather because he knew he had pushed himself too hard for too long. He won, with an increased per cent of the vote. A celebration dinner for our workers had become a matter of form and it took place on 19th May 1979. We had a Conservative government and Margaret Thatcher as Prime Minister now, and our only cause for sadness was that Rt Hon Airey Neave, who had been cruelly assassinated, would not be Secretary of State for Northern Ireland. A man of tremendous ability had been lost to us and we felt it personally.

At Westminster, instead of feeling guilty about having a free hour or two on his hands between debates or committees, Robert began to go to concerts or a show and tried to relax mid-week.

Our two-week summer holiday in Corfu was a disaster: we arrived on a Monday and Claire was very tired, but by Tuesday I knew it was more than tiredness. It was *measles*! Robert and I spent the whole first week taking it in turns to go to the beach and it was a very thin, frail, white little girl that emerged onto the beach for the second week. Our tiny villa in an orange grove was lovely but isolated and it was a long hot walk to the village to shop. This was our first experience of the Greeks and we couldn't get over their friendliness. If we bought groceries the grocer would shut his shop and take off to the villa on his motorbike with Robert riding pillion, a carrier bag in each hand trying to hold himself on with his knees. The grocer would then deliver Robert back to the village and we were free to wander around and eat a meal without our heavy parcels. Food was very cheap and rather exciting. If you were interested, the restaurant owners, were quite happy for you to wander into their kitchens and point to what you wanted to eat.

Home again, hardly feeling refreshed from what amounted to a week's holiday, it was immediately back to the grindstone. The summer recess, I always felt, should be slightly less hectic than the rest of the year, but it never seemed to work out that way. Robert called August the 'silly season,' when news drifted by on a euphoric cloud. But there were just as many housing problems, perhaps a few less appointments being made but still little time for us as a family to spend a day together. If we stayed in the house someone would phone or call with an urgent problem that had to be dealt with there and then. So the only solution was to go out for the day.

Moral legislation such as trying to prevent laws being passed to make abortion easy, was taking up an increasing amount of Robert's time and thinking. Life was sacred to Robert as to his Lord and he fought hard every inch of the way. Pornography was another forte. He became almost physically ill at some of the filth he was sent, such magazines a father sent . . .

'My eleven year-old son bought this in our local newsagent.' And many other such instances. In the case of a library book that gave graphic details of a child molestation he instructed a lawyer to take action to get it withdrawn from public library shelves.

'I will pursue this to high court action if necessary, whatever the cost,' he announced to the press.

Late in August I had blocked off three days in Robert's diary, determined that he should take a short break before winter came in in earnest. Having enjoyed Killarney so much we thought we would chance Galway. To stay in northern Ireland was not a holiday because we only had to walk down a street or road, and in the space of a couple of hundred yards three or four people would have stopped him and each had along chat. Robert enjoyed this up to a point, but I got fed-up very quickly. It was a thrill for people to talk to their MP and Robert realising it, didn't like to seem rude.

We got as far as Enniskillen for the week-end and Robert decided he had to go back to Belfast for half a day. The friends we were staying with were going to Mullaghmore to water-ski, so Claire and I joined them. It was a beautiful bright summer's day, hardly a wisp of cloud in the blue sky as we drove into the tiny village. But what was all the commotion and the ambulances and the Guarda? The people we had been travelling to be with had gone out in their boat as we were late arriving, and had been nearby as Lord Louis Mountbatten and his family had been assassinated by terrorists who had blown up his boat. They and some others had managed to haul the bodies and some survivors to shore.

The awful state of shock that our friends were in emphas-

ised what an unbelievable nightmare had shaken that beautiful day into unforgettable blackness. It was as if the sun
had ceased to shine even though I could see its light and feel
its heat. Just a few more hideous notches on a depraved
terrorist's gun. The police advised us that Galway would not
be a good idea so we came home, cheated out of yet another
break.

'Let's go to London.' Robert suggested and although it
was like a busman's holiday for him we went. The heat-wave
continued and we tried to relax with the tide of revulsion
flowing all around us at the cruel end to such a gracious
man's life.

We spoke with English accents for those few days as we
walked the streets sightseeing. We knew we dare not let it
be known that we were from Northern Ireland for fear of
being lynched from the nearest lamp-post as terrorists. Yet
we had to live through this war as victims with no real way
of fighting back adequately. Men, women and children
were being cut down for some senseless long-forgotten
cause. The mindless violence had become a way of life for
the terrorists who obviously spent their time thinking up
more and more dastardly deeds to commit, each one more
depraved than the last. Robert and I both felt that the only
real solution to the problem was the return of our Saviour
Jesus Christ. But we are told by him to *'Occupy till I come'* –
so it was back to political life.

Robert worked hard at achieving Unionist unity. He
managed with difficulty to remain in close contact with all
brands of Unionism and constantly tried to draw his own,
and other Unionist parties, closer together. The logical next
step was to put his name forward as possible leader of his
own Official Unionist Party. In an interview in the Belfast
Newsletter he stated his reasons:

> *'I am not an integrationist although I concede that this
> course might be seen as a logical extension of Unionism.
> Because it is clear that we cannot really entrust our future
> in terms of security, to either of the major parties at West-
> minster, I could not lead the party into an integrationist
> situation.'*

About Unionist unity he stated:

> '*I think it is counter-productive always to be seen to be either reacting to, or provoking misunderstandings on, misconceptions within the Unionist family. I would like to see an improved relationship within Unionism in Northern Ireland and an end to the sterile dogfights and perpetual conflicts. I believe we should have a relationship with those parties who want to maintain the Union.*' (with Britain)

Together we had discussed what leadership would mean in terms of time and commitment. Robert said,

'I will have to spend a lot of time travelling around Ulster, speaking to the various branches, but I feel by doing that I could draw them all closer together. It will take considerable extra time and effort but many Unionist people feel that I could do the party a lot of good. I'm certainly willing to give my all.'

Robert did not get the leadership and I was very relieved; I felt the extra pressure would have been unbearable from my point of view.

It was the Thursday before Christmas and Robert's last trip to London for 1979. He had to catch the early flight to be there for his various committees. 'Wee Jimmy' was always up by six a.m. so Robert asked him to transport him to the airport to save us taking Claire out of her bed so early.

The car hadn't left for more than half an hour when I heard a vehicle drive down the driveway. I looked out the basement window and realised it was them coming back.

'What's wrong?' I asked at the door.

'We had an accident; make us a cup of tea, Mum's a bit shaken.'

'Any of you hurt?' I inquired anxiously, there was steam rising from the bashed car's radiator.

'No, we're all fine, there was no-one else involved.' Robert sat down. 'We were travelling down Blacks Road to go over Colin Mountain to the airport, and at the last curve the car just took off. I wasn't going fast because it was so icy but it was like the dodgems. We sailed across the road and hit a Granada Estate car parked in a layby, bounced off, spun round and up the grass slope on the opposite side of the road, slid down back across the road again. This time we hit a Volvo in the same layby. The car finally came to standstill and we got out to find we couldn't stand, the road was a complete sheet of black ice.'

'I suppose everyone was out of their houses?'

'Not a sinner appeared and I didn't want to start knocking doors at than unearthly hour to find out who the owners were.'

'You didn't just leave?' I said aghast.

'No, of course not. I called in at the Police Barracks and told them what had happened and asked them, when the owners came in, to give them my phone number.' I made some breakfast and we waited for the inevitable phone calls. It was nine o'clock before the phone rang. Robert grabbed the receiver.

'Yes I'm terribly sorry . . . black ice, the car took off, my insurance will cover it. By the way, when your neighbour discovers his car tell him . . . you own both?' Robert gasped then held his nose to smother his laughter.

'I promise you the air in Blacks Road was very blue this morning Mr Bradford, I've had this happen several times, usually with hit and run drunken drivers. I went to put the key in the door of my Volvo to find it caved in, so I said a few choice words and I thought, it's as well I hired the Granada Estate for this week. I walked to it and I'll not repeat what I said then!' Robert could not restrain his laughter at this point. He apologised again, told the man to hire a car and he would cover the cost of it and hung up. Robert could not contain himself.

'He owns both,' he wiped his eyes as he laughed, 'can't you just see that poor man's face when he walked out of his house this morning?' and he was off into convulsions of laughter again.

The general monotony of life went on for the next few days when Claire decided to confine us to the house with mumps. I phoned Robert in London as he was about to leave for home.

'Great,' he said, 'that means we can have roast lamb instead of turkey and there'll be just ourselves. We can take the phone off the hook and have a lovely quiet time together over Christmas.'

We had applied to adopt another child and although it came as no surprise to be refused, it was still hard news to take; Robert took it hardest. It was a difficult time for us both but I watched him withdraw into himself as life weighed him down yet further.

As the battle raged on between Robert and the IRA, he continued in his efforts to make people more aware of their fund-raising activities. He knew they were closing in, but we had confidence in our God that he was able to keep us safe until his appointed time . . . 'for I know whom I have believed and am persuaded that he is able to keep what I have commited to him until that day.' (2 Timothy 1, 12 RAV). We took every precaution possible but were fully aware that some morning we could open the front door or the garage door and be blown up by a bomb hung there by a meat hook – as this was their latest devilish device. The terrorists wouldn't care if they killed Robert or me or Claire or all three. They had no thought that while Robert used democratic means to fight for what he felt was right for Ulster, they, knowing they couldn't win by such fair means, had long ago resorted to foul. They wanted to silence all dissenting voices.

By the summer we decided to chance another holiday in Corfu.

Near the end of our stay we hired a car to tour the island, stopping first in Corfu town to buy presents for the family at home. The narrow picturesque streets intrigued us and we wandered up and down gazing at shop windows. Robert was walking in front while Claire and I sauntered a long behind holding hands. The street was deserted, being siesta time. A solitary, tall, well-dressed, Greek came by waving his arms. As he passed us he deliberately hit Claire a whack on the ear.

'What do you think you're doing?' I shouted after him as I gathered the frightened child into my arms. Robert turned on his heel and saw Claire with tears beginning to roll down her white startled face.

'He just hit her for no reason,' I said.

Robert chased after him shouting.

'What did you do that for?' As Robert got level the man swung on his heel and grabbed Robert in a bear-hug, pinning his arms by his side. Struggle as he might Robert couldn't free himself. The deranged man then sunk his teeth into Robert's neck at his jugular vein and bit hard. I put Claire in a doorway and ran down the street. I tried to pull Robert free with no effect. I was frantic. I scraped my rings hard down the man's cheek, he stopped biting and still holding on to Robert he lashed out sideways and kicked me hard. The shopkeepers poured into the street and dragged the man off. He ran away quickly leaving us all terribly shaken, not really understanding what had happened. The man had been shouting about his team losing a football match, the locals explained. And they confirmed that although immaculately dressed they regarded him as totally mad. They took us to a chemist shop to get Robert's neck dressed and I thought of what might have been the fatal consequences if this 'vampire' had indeed managed to pierce Robert's jugular vein.

The shopkeepers pleaded with us to report the incident to the tourist board as it would help them but the last thing Robert wanted was to be headline news.

I stored the incident away wondering why such a force of evil had been unleashed on Robert. About a month later at home I had a strange dream which I related to him.

> *'I was standing in a town square and for no apparent reason I was attacked by a black man and you came running to help me. The black man drew a knife and stabbed you. I woke up terrified, seeing myself cradling your head in my arms, not knowing if you were alive or dead.'*

We didn't know what to make of such a strange dream and thought it was probably an aftermath of the Corfu incident.

Robert's next visit to the USA was to include Claire and me. The first week we had arranged to spend with Florence and Webb and they had decided to show us New Orleans. We were to fly out on Thursday morning, but Wednesday night Robert phoned from London with some bad news. Although it was almost recess, a vote of confidence in Margaret Thatcher had been called and he would have to stay behind. Claire and I flew to Vicksburg alone.

New Orleans was fascinating, though to walk the streets in one hundred degrees F. was hardly a pleasure. I love heat, but not that much. It was all very interesting but I was aware of the undercurrent of another life there, that revolved around drugs, drink, and depravity, and was not sorry to leave. We picked Robert up at the airport on the way back to Vicksburg.

Claire went to camp with Vicksburg church young people for the next week while Robert and I went on to Monticello for another revival. We stayed in a trailer beside the manse for this visit which we found very relaxing and I became quite good at cooking American biscuits (scones) for breakfast. Dr Sellers said he could tell when we were up by the pop from the can of biscuits as I broke them open.

The Sellers discovered that Robert had missed seeing New Orleans and left Wednesday free to take us there. Robert was apprehensive for he felt it wasn't right to be gallivanting in the middle of a Mission. He would rather have worked at his sermon but he couldn't be rude to our hosts. Wednesday came and we dressed in light clothes for the heat and our host drove us down.

The Football Superdome was what really thrilled Robert – it's gigantic size with tier upon tier of seats. The large central screens for instant action replays, the plush rooms and press boxes, everything was on such a vast scale as to be almost incomprehensible.

'The air conditioning has to be constantly on,' we were told by the guide, 'because clouds would actually form inside the stadium otherwise.'

We went back into town for lunch and in the crush I bumped into a large black man,

'Sorry,' I said and stepped back.

He smiled nastily and said something crude. Robert didn't quite catch the words but he got the look on my face.

'What did he say?' he asked obviously angry.

Into my mind instantly flashed my dream.

'It doesn't matter, *remember my dream*!' I warned.

Robert stopped and studied me for a minute. Looking back I was convinced that man would have thought nothing of knifing Robert and that Satan had it set up, but his time was not yet, so God had warned us by the dream to be on our guard. The second Mission took place in Greenville with the Geralds as our hosts, and that was a real treat. Then inevitably came the time for home.

As winter's cold enveloped us, the threats were still rolling in week by week as Robert worked at compiling more and more information, delivered sometimes from the strangest sources, on the IRA's activities. He was fighting a lonely battle with a few of the other elected MPs prepared to stand out so strongly. They were all too fully aware of the consequences of such action. The threats only made Robert all the more determined. He appeared week after week on each channel of the TV, feeling he had to keep the public aware of the progress he was making, or lack of it. He could be at either TV studio in a very few minutes, so with his ability to give a quick, concise and helpful statement, it meant he was always in demand for a comment on the latest atrocity, and there were a growing number of actrocities to comment on.

A full-time police guard, David, was assigned to Robert as the year drew to a close. David fitted in with us very well and we felt it a special blessing that we had been assigned a committed Christian. It was difficult to adjust to having someone constantly with us but David made his presence as unobtrusive as possible.

Robert's plans for a full-time office had begun to take shape and a couple of room above a shop on the Cregagh Road were rented. I set to to make the curtains and Robert went out and bought extra desks, chairs and filing cabinets. It was all organised by Christmas and it was arranged to transfer our phone number in January. This was done very quickly and instead of the phone calls we would generally have had all over the holidays we found they were already being transferred to the empty office.

Just before Christmas, my friend Christine and I had arranged an evening out together. We drove down town and parked in a little alley near the city centre and went for a meal. We hadn't been away more than an hour when we returned to find the car had been stolen.

The police gave us little hope as they felt it was probably joy riders, the latest craze. I visualised our new light blue Granada wrapped around a lamp-post.

David collected Robert from the airport in his own car and Robert was rather quiet when he arrived.

'What happened?' he asked as he kissed me.

'It just went – Chris and I parked it and came back in an hour and it was gone.

And please don't tell me that alley is notorious for car thefts. I have been told that by everyone but no-on saw fit to tell me before hand.'

'It's only a car,' Robert soothed me, 'there are a lot worse things that could have happened.'

The police phoned to say it had been spotted in Anders-town, a Republican strong-hold. That was hardly surprising as nearly all the joy-riding was done from there.

'We think they may have discovered it was your car Sir,' the policeman said.

Robert's preaching gowns were in the boot in a case with his name on it.

'Then don't let anyone go near it,' Robert pleaded, I'd rather you blew it up, it's bound to be booby trapped.'

A short time later we heard the unmistakeable sound of our car being driven into the basement garage. The police had checked it out, then one of them had got in and started it up. The very thought of it brought me out in goose pimples – he could have been blown to kingdom come.

We thanked him profusely and after it was finger-printed I set to scrubbing out the interior where the thieves had made a real mess. There were milk bottles on the back seat half full of petrol as if they had been disturbed making petrol bombs. There was little damage to the body work and we felt we had got off lightly. Our next step was to get a trip switch fitted.

'A bit like bolting the door after the horse has gone,' I thought.

The new office was advertised by leaflets through our constituents' doors and the house became very quiet with only our friends having our private phone number. Kaye, Robert's secretary seemed to enjoy the office routine and the company of the extra two part-time girls Robert took on to answer the phone, take appointments and do some filing.

Robert had worked out a system for constituents problems, where if he had no satisfactory answer in a short time the issues was brought to his attention again. He was on good terms with the Housing Officers for the Housing Executive and his success rate for solving constituents problems was high.

We were all, as a family, very fond of Chinese food and regularly visited various Chinese restaurants. Over the years through this habit we had got to know quite a few of Belfast's Chinese community. A long time ago Robert had discovered that they were being charged astronomical prices by a solicitor for writing letters for them, and Robert began

144

to write their letters and help them with their problems.

The Chinese folk had frequently mentioned taking us to Hong Kong for a holiday but Robert had always refused on the grounds that it might be looked on as a bribe. He consulted a few friends at Westminster and decided it was only a gift for work done and he finally said 'yes' to Mr Tsang. I was overjoyed as I was to be included. Robert felt there was a lot of money floating around Hong Kong and perhaps he could encourage some of it to be invested in Ulster or Great Britain.

The flight out for our eight-day trip that Easter had its usual collapse case . . . I had my miniature brandy in my pocket and administered a small amount quickly with the usual good effect. Thankfully our Chinese companion was asleep at the time and no fuss was created. The episode surprised us both because since his last spell in hospital Robert had been taking more rest and sleeping better. For the first time I really emphasised how bad I felt Robert's condition to be and insisted that he see a specialist when we got home. He made the usual promises and I knew he hadn't the slightest intention of keeping.

Hong Kong was all bright lights and clamour. A fascinating place where everything was done at high speed. The only leisurely times were meals and they could take hours. They were really interesting, with from six to ten courses, and even though we only nibbled with chop-sticks we often found it hard to finish. Thankfully those meals were few or our weight problems would have got really out of hand!

Our hosts made sure we saw as much of Hong Kong in our short stay as possible, even devising a scheme to get us close to the border with China. The whole visit was a very memorable one and Robert made some interesting business contacts.

For a long time Robert had been watching out for a chance of a flat close to Parliament. He saw two that he liked the look of. He phoned as usual one evening to discuss them and described them in detail. They both sounded lovely but I advised the third floor one as opposed to the first floor one. 'People will notice too readily on the first floor, that you are away every week-end, and it's also less likely that terrorists could stage a sniper bid on the third floor.'

The third floor flat it was, and it was with great excitement that we got the keys and walked in. It was going to require a lot of redecorating but it was lovely planning it all.

We had a week in Devon booked in August and we thought we would spend the subsequent week decorating the flat in London.

We drove through the Republic of Ireland to take the short ferry crossing to Wales. Robert was very tired so when we landed in Wales I took over and drove. It was after midnight and the lights were on in all the bed-and-breakfast houses near the quayside. I felt reasonably fresh and thought I could drive on down to the South of England and we could have an extra day there. Robert and Claire slept as I drove along the narrow windy Welsh roads and on to the motorways. It was about four in the morning as I was driving through the rain and fog that the lights suddenly dimmed and went out, windscreen wipers slowed, the fan stopped and the car ground to a halt. I sat for a minute in astonishment, then tried to start it again. Nothing doing. I shook Robert to wake him.

'The car's conked out.'

'Fine dear,' he smiled sleepily and promptly went back to sleep.

'Oh well' I thought, 'not much point in trying him again. Might only be a fuse.'

I lifted the bonnet, located the fuse box and lifted out one after another but they all seemed fine. I tried the car again, it started!

'Nothing short of genius,' I congratulated myself, closed the bonnet and drove on, both passengers still sound asleep. It was six o'clock when we got to Devon. I parked near the seafront and we all snoozed until a hotel opened so that we could get some breakfast.

The weather stayed dry and mild for us as we spent the first day on the beach. We had only been there two days when the news of the death of Robert's sister was phoned through to us. Robert took the train to London and flew home for the funeral. When he arrived back he was obviously more tense and as the week went on he seemed less and less able to relax. We drove to London and set to to decorate the newly acquired flat. We had brought lilos and sleeping bags for the first days until we could purchase some

146

furniture, but when we went to blow up the large one for us we found the bung was missing. We spent a dreadful night on a knotted wood floor and first thing next morning searched until we found a cut-price furniture establishment that would deliver a single and a double bed that day.

By the end of the week we were both very weary. We had worked very hard and although we had gone out a few times, by the time we were to leave, Robert and I felt we needed a holiday. Robert's back had completely seized up and I ended up driving the whole way to the ferry.

Robert was soon to head off to Mississippi for another preaching tour. I was very frightened about him flying on his own, though perhaps because he didn't totally relax when on his own he didn't seem to have bother as often. 'I try not to sleep when I'm on my own and I promise to keep some brandy at hand.' Robert found brandy hard to take but if he watered it down he found he could sip at it and make it last almost the whole six to eight hour flight. He phoned when he arrived to assure me he was well. Preaching was his life-blood and I knew he would really enjoy this trip.

He was hardly home when an idea for a political trip to the USA to tell the true Ulster story began to take shape and so 'Operation USA' was born. He decided it should be undertaken properly with Public Relations Officers and widespread publicity, but the main problem was finance. Funds would have to be raised. John Taylor and Dr Paisley showed an interest in the idea and they decided on a United Unionist Delegation.

Robert felt it would be good to include some lay representatives on the trip but that didn't work out. While all this was taking shape Robert was off on another trip to Hong Kong. This time I couldn't go as it was school term time for Claire.

As always Robert phoned immediately he arrived to tell me how the flight went and that he was fine. It was only a short eight-day trip again but he was hoping to get financial backing for a redevelopment project in London. He was also meeting more and more of the Hong Kong Chinese community with a view to encouraging all kinds of investments for home.

Robert had written to the Hong Kong High Commissioner and he managed to obtain an interview. He came home really feeling he was making some progress.

For Robert it was back to the grindstone in London and into session in the House of Commons. By now he was very familiar with the history of that great Palace of Westminster where the two houses of Parliament sit. The House of Commons being a totally elected body and the House of Lords comprising of Peers of the Realm, the Lords 'Spiritual', the Bishops of the Church of England and the Lords 'Temporal.'

It was a great delight to him to give guided tours to school groups from N. Ireland. He paraded them through the vast complex making history really come alive with a fund of funny stories about the characters that lived long ago. Constituents or friends who called would be admitted through the St Stephens entrance, then make their way to the Strangers lobby and send a 'green card' into the House of Commons to let Robert know they had arrived.

The pomp and solemnity with which everything there was carried out appealed to Robert. The stately procession from the Speakers chambers to the House of Commons for prayers at 2.30 pm was carried out with extreme dignity. At times when standing quietly in the crowd he was tempted to spoil the solemnity of the procession by shouting 'walkies' but his sense of regard for the Speaker and reverence for the stately traditions always held him back.

The area that the public have access to is only a small part of that vast complex. It also housed offices, restaurants, numerous bars, a hairdresser, a gymnasium and a travel agents. It was known for MPs who had been there several years still to get lost. It really was a thrill for me to go behind the scenes. My favourite place was the balcony which overlooked the grubby Thames. Somehow the grime of the river didn't matter when you sat out there under the green striped awnings of the House of Commons tent and ate the luscious strawberries from the dish in front of you, watching the slow river traffic pass and listening to Big Ben chime.

The Christian prayer group usually met on Wednesday at 2.30 pm. These were times that Robert really enjoyed, with a nucleus of ten to twelve members attending it remained a very intimate group of believing people who prayed and read the Scriptures together.

The debates in the House were rather more tedious, especially Northern Ireland business. That was the sign for most people to vacate the chamber. In all the years he had been there this never ceased to amaze Robert. We had a terrorist war going on and the other MPs weren't even prepared to stay and listen to the debate.

The ancient method of voting through the 'Aye' and 'No' lobbies is still regarded throughout the world as foolproof. When a divisional vote is called the members file towards the lobby of their choice. 'ayes' to the Speakers right and the 'Nos' to his left. Their names are ticked off as they pass a desk, then two tellers, one from the Government and one from the Opposition also count heads. In the early days of 1974 when the loyalist eleven were first elected, by their combined numbers they had immense power over that 'hung Parliament.' They could sway a vote either way. The major parties spent long hours wooing them but they stuck firmly together and used that power to their best advantage. Northern Ireland business was usually debated into the small hours in those days and Robert was very tired of those late night into early morning sittings. He decided he would like a better attendance of MPs so in the early hours he and some others called for a vote and then took great delight in watching the various MPs who had to drag themselves out of their beds to come and vote at that unearthly hour of the morning.

Those early days in Parliament seemed a lifetime away now but looking back Robert wondered how after all Ulster had been through, despite the combined effort of all the loyalist MPs, many stirring speeches from himself and others, the war was still continuing. If anything the terrorists were gaining momentum. Nothing seemed to have the least effect on that gathered body of elected representatives. Even Rt Hon Airey Neave's cold-blooded assassination had faded into history. No-one in London seemed to appreciate just how sinister an enemy we were up against, much less how to deal with them.

Terrorists were now murdering at least one member of the security forces each day. The death toll was rising at an unbelievable rate. There was a funeral to be attended practically every day.

'If I have to go to one more bereaved home and get asked once again what the Government is doing and not be able to say anything helpful, I think I'll crack,' Robert said as he took of his black light-weight wool overcoat that I called his 'funeral coat,' for he rarely wore it anywhere else. The effect of walking behind yet another coffin with the police band playing the 'Death Knoll' or attending again a UDR Military funeral, was devastating for Robert.

But the news the next day was the same, and so too the day after.

The pressure was really telling on me now also. At work I would walk down a corridor and totally forget what I had gone for and finally when I was asked to pull myself together, I went to see my doctor.

'I'm just not coping, and I can't see any way around it,' I told him.

He ordered me a month off work and prescribed some mild tranquillisers.

I felt very guilty sitting at home, especially as I thought in a month's time our position would be no different – I would simply *have* to gather all the threads of my life together and try to carry on.

I woke very early and, not wanting to wake Robert, I went upstairs with a book and read until about eight a.m. Then I went back to bed. Robert woke, smiled at me and said,

'You OK?'

'Just couldn't sleep, so I went upstairs to read.'

We chatted for a while and Robert himself was very depressed so the conversation came around to our present tense situation.

'You've wasted ten years of your life being married to me,' he said. You could have married someone really nice and been very happy.'

'I wanted to marry you,' I said.

'I know, that's very precious to me.'

He got up, washed and started dressing. He had yet another funeral to go to that Saturday morning. He took his light grey suit out of the wardrobe and I thought he'd forgotten.

'You've Mr Bell's funeral this morning, don't forget, your black suit's ironed.'

'My overcoat will cover it. I don't want to walk around in black all day.'

'Are your wearing clerics or your black tie?'

He didn't answer as he proceeded to take his favourite spotted maroon tie out of the drawer. It was the one that Claire had bought for him.

I jumped anxiously out of bed to search for his black tie. He took it from me without speaking and looked at it for a minute. Then he rolled it up and put it in his pocket.

'I'll put it on after the advice centre.' It was a while before David arrived to escort Robert. Robert pottered around the house obviously with a heavy heart and even when David arrived he didn't leave immediately.

'He's never going to get away from the advice centre for the funeral at eleven thirty if he doesn't leave soon,' I thought.

I went to the front door to let the dogs have a romp on the grass and stood watching that they didn't venture on to the road. Our 'silly tree' was just loosing its leaves. I walked over to it and had an irresistible urge to tie on those last remaining three leaves.

'You really are nuts' I scolded myself.

Back into my mind flashed a childhood story I had read of a little black boy called Joe. His little friend was very ill and she had decided that when the last leaves left the tree outside her bedroom window she would depart for heaven. Joe climbed the tree in the dark and with his shoe laces he tied on three leaves. His little friend drew courage when the leaves didn't blow away in the wind and lived.

Robert called 'Bye love' from the garage door and I hastened out to get the dogs in in case the departing car should hit them.

The estate surrounding the community centre where the advice centre was being held was being painted, so two men in boiler suits carrying a short plank didn't attract much attention until they were close beside David and Ken Campbell standing in the doorway. Pulling guns from behind the plank, they made both lie face down and then shot Ken. One stayed there while two others raced into the building where a children's disco was in full swing, and some people were queued up to see Robert.

The elderly couple with Robert didn't have time to turn

as before their eyes he was assasinated in his chair. The first
shot rendered him instantly unconscious and the next six
were presumably for good measure. They didn't know that
seven is God's number of perfection or that the day they
chose for their dastardly deed, November 14th would be a
seal from my God that he had allowed this to happen.

The phone rang and a close friend told me there had been
some trouble at the advice centre.

'Please stay there, I'll be straight over,' Bill said.

I gathered Claire on to my knee and told he she was going
to have to be very brave, but I thought that Daddy had been
hurt. We put on our coats and were just about to leave in
some vain attempt to get to Robert when David arrived.

'Which hospital have they taken him to?' I called as I
raced up the driveway.

'Come inside a minute,' he pleaded, pulling me towards
the door.

'You're wasting time,' I thought. 'I need to get to him,' I
said aloud.

He shook his head and tears welled into his eyes as he
continued to pull me towards the house. I shook my head,
my knees were giving way but I fought to stand. The words
wouldn't come out. I managed,

'You mean . . . gone,' I sobbed.

He nodded, tears streaming down his face.

'We can resuscitate him!' I took fresh courage.

He shook his head again and I allowed him to bring me
inside. We sat on the sofa and he gently went over what had
happened. I knew he was in no state to talk it over but I had
to know. I wasn't even conscious that Claire was on my knee
until she spoke.

'You mean my Daddy's been shot?'

I came down to earth with a bump . . . I hugged her,
realising that the full significance of it all hadn't really sunk
in for her . . . It was a bit like cowboys and indians, when
shot they always got up and ran on. I looked at David and
realised how dreadful he looked. I had seen him so often
watch other cars as we stopped at traffic lights. On visits to
Suffolk or other dangerous areas I had seen him place himself bodily on the side that sniper fire was likely to come
from to shield Robert. He was no Starsky or Hutch, just a
'copper' doing the job he had been assigned to to the best of

his ability.

'Don't blame yourself,' I offered.

'But I do!' he said jumping up and pacing the room,' surely I could have done more!'

'If you could you would have,' and I meant it for I knew him well, 'you're no use to your family dead, you know you couldn't have saved him from four of them.'

The house filled with people very quickly. My family arrived, arms laden with food to feed the massing crowds. They took over the kitchen and tea was poured by the gallon. I phoned Sadie and Jimmy to come over urgently. I didn't want to tell them on the phone. I went to the door as they parked their car. How could I tell them? I looked at my 'silly tree.' There was just one leaf left, but a tiny precious white blossom had burst open.

'That's my Lord,' I thought, 'only he would give me such a beautiful sign of his love. 'To show me that where earthly life ends, a heavenly and more glorious life begins for those who know him as their personal Saviour. Like a caterpillar turning into a butterfly, so Robert had been transported into another realm.

'Thank you for to-day,' I prayed, 'I don't understand, but I know you allowed it to happen. I know I have to thank you in faith and that someday I will know why.'

It seemed the whole of Ulster was sitting on a knife edge. Even in my state of shock I could feel the extreme tension. I felt it would take very little to make the lid blow off. Only the high regard with which Robert was held by everyone and the knowledge that he strived so long for peace stopped a retaliatory backlash. News of Robert's death had been flashed around the world. Friends in Australia and America were on the phone within hours having heard it on their own news broadcasts. Missionaries in far outposts wept for the loss of a friend. Telegrams streamed into the house as did the people, Protestant and Catholic. The phone went non-stop, messages from all across the spectrum. The carnage didn't stop though, there was a report of another UDR man being killed, obviously to try to burst the banks of the river of emotion that was rocking the province.

An Ulster lady penned this verse.

One Death Too Many

How many more will have to die
Before this war is won,
Does Ulster's blood not matter,
Must we lose another son?

Would the English be so patient,
If these deaths had happened there,
Do they think we're living normal lives
Or do they really care?

What use is Britain's army
If they need a yellow card,
So they can shoot a terrorist
For whom no holds are barred?

Is no-one going to help us
To end this bitter fight,
We've lost a fearless Ulsterman
Whose priorities were right

Let's make a fitting tribute
To a man who gave his all-
We have got to be united
For divided we shall fall.

Lilian Ross.

The funeral was set for Tuesday. Robert and I had discussed his funeral arrangements for we both knew in our hearts that it was only a matter of time. I organised it as he had requested even though I had threatened him at the time that I would do it my way as he wouldn't be in any position to object.

In forty cities, towns and villages throughout Ulster memorial services were planned for Tuesday lunch-time to coincide with Robert's funeral service in Dundonald Presbyterian Church. These memorial services had a multiple purpose. To remember Robert; to lay wreaths for all the police, UDR and civilians that had been killed in this and previous wars; to protest at the Government's security policy in Ulster and perhaps most important, to go to God for release of the unutterable anguish in so many hearts. Many tributes to Robert were printed in the death columns of the newspapers. One read, 'Greater love hath no man than that he lay down his life for his friends.'

Fifteen thousand attended the Belfast City centre service at the cenotaph. Shops and offices closed for an hour to allow employees to attend. Traffic ground to a halt as crowds spilled over onto the streets. Workers from Harland and Wolff Shipbuilders and Shorts Planemakers marched four abreast in their thousands through the Belfast streets headed by a Union Jack and some wreath bearers, to pay their tribute.

Throughout Ulster at least seventy five thousand people met quietly and with great dignity at various war memorials and town squares where they sang hymns, held two minutes silence and joined in anxious prayers to God for our beloved country. Their numbers represented one in ten of the adult working population of Ulster.

Flags flew at half mast over the countryside. As I travelled to Dundonald for the funeral the roads were quiet and deserted as if it were a Sunday morning. I felt the grief of the whole people come down upon me as I sat in that black limousine as it smoothly and silently took me on my way. I had the feeling if there had been cranes along the route they would have bowed as they had for Sir Winston Churchill's funeral. so great was Ulster's feeling of loss.

When I reached Dundonald the crowds were already stretching far along the road. The church itself was already packed to capacity with people crammed into the foyer and stairs. I entered by a side door and took my seat.

The coffin was decked with the Ulster flag, the Red Cross of Saint Patrick on a white background, which was the emblem of Robert's Orange Lodge. On top lay the bunch of flowers Claire had picked from her Grannie's garden and sent for her Dad. The cross-shaped wreath of red carnations and roses from me was beside it. Other numerous wreaths were already on the cars to go straight to the cemetery.

Rev. Roy Magee led a service of praise and glory to God for his infinite mercy and love. A love that I already felt enveloped in, and was to be supported by, for many long days to come.

As we came out into the clear brisk chilly day the roads were lined with the vast numbers of people that had gathered outside the church to listen to the service as it was relayed by loudspeaker. School children lined their school fencing, crowds of silent people stood as the hearse containing Robert's earthly shell moved to its resting place. The cars quickened as we left Dundonald and when we hit Newtownards there were more crowds. Policemen controlling the crowds saluted as the hearse passed, some with tears rolling down their cheeks.

'Wee Jimmy' and some others carried the coffin the short distance to the open grave and the final service began. The people listened quietly to the words of hope while a trawler anchored respectfully in the bay by local fishermen rolled gently in the quiet sea. The stillness was as if the hand of God was laid on us saying,

> *'Be still and know that I am God.'*

I went to stay with my Mum to be alone for a few days. The following Saturday was an horrific day for me as I relived every moment of the previous one.

I stood alone in the cemetery, weeping silently, trying to understand. I turned my back on the quiet mound of red clay covered with flowers and the sun warmed my face.

> *'As Judas Iscariot had a part to play in the crucifixion of Jesus Christ but was insignificant in my final plan, so the terrorists had a part to play in Robert's death, but are as unimportant to my mighty purpose.'*

I stood very still allowing it to sink in slowly.

My God was speaking to me. The all-powerful King of heaven had stooped to whisper in my ear. I went on my way with tears of joy in my eyes.

Some months later God put another seal on the life of Robert by the verse he gave me as an inscription for Robert's headstone:

156

'A lovely fragrance, a sacrifice that pleases the very heart of God.'

(Philippians 4.18, J. B. Phillips)

Robert's job was done. His time on this earth had come to an end but a more glorious life was just beginning, and that will last for all Eternity.

Thank you God, for releasing Robert to stroll gently through the City paved with gold beside his blessed Saviour.

'A lovely fragrance, a sacrifice that pleases the very heart of God.'

EPILOGUE

In the difficult days that followed that Saturday I was given tremendous encouragement from the Scriptures. On the night of that 14th November 1981 in Daily Light my reading was,

> 'Though I walk through the valley of the shadow of death, I will fear no evil: for thou art with me; thy rod and thy staff they comfort me. – Ps. 23v4. When thou passest through the waters, I will be with thee; and through the rivers, they shall not overflow thee. -Is. 43v2.
> Fear not; I am the first and the last: I am he that liveth, and was dead; and behold, I am alive for evermore. Amen; and have the keys of hell and of death. - Rev. lv17,18.'
> (Daily Light).

And similarly the next morning,

> 'Rejoice, inasmuch as ye are partakers of Christ's sufferings; that, when his glory shall be revealed, ye may be glad also with exceeding joy. – 1 Peter 4v13.'
> (Daily Light)

A week later as I relived the 14th my Daily Light quoted,

> 'I will remember my covenant with thee in the days of thy youth, and I will establish unto thee an everlasting covenant. – Ezekiel 16v60
> A bruised reed shall he not break, and the smoking flax shall he not quench.' Is.42v3'

I came back from the cemetery where God had spoken to me feeling such a mixture of emotions. Again the scriptures spoke,

> His dear Son – Col 1v13
> The glory which thou gavest me I have given them; that they may be one, even as we are one: I in them, and thou in me, that they may know that thou hast sent me, and hast

158

loved them, as thou hast loved me. — John 17v22–24.
Behold, what manner of love the Father hath bestowed
upon us, that we should be called the sons of God. — I
John 3v1.'

As the days stretched into weeks I felt the presence of the
Lord so close to me. The prayers of hundreds, perhaps
thousands of people bore me along several inches off the
ground.

Memories crowded back from the past. Tiny incidents
long forgotten rushed forward and reduced me sometimes
to laughter, more often to tears. I threw myself into sorting
out Robert's office and answering the hundreds of letters of
sympathy. It was easy to be busy during the day but the
nights were interminable. Christmas was looming up large
on my horizon as an unsurmountable hurdle. How was I
ever going to face it? It was going to need something special
to get me through this festive family week, so the Lord sent
an ambassador. Roberta Clements, armed with her record
'Open my eyes Lord' arrived on my doorstep on Christmas
Eve. Through that Spirit filled music and her friendship,
God gave me the strength to go forward once again with my
hand in his mighty grasp.

A month later when I finally came out of shock, I hit rock
bottom. But even at the bottom of that deep, deep pit I
found Jesus Christ. He had been there before me. Again he
sent help in my dark hours of need.

It is now over two years since that Saturday in November
1981. God has never failed me in all that time. I have often
failed him but when I look to him again he stretches out his
patient loving hands and lifts me up again, sets my feet
upon firmer ground and points the way forward.

He has brought me through the fire that I may be refined
as pure gold and has taught me that those whom he loves he
chastens. Only by the sufferings I have been allowed to
endure can I become a fit vessel for his use. Only by having
been there myself can I help others to come through the
refining fire and become as 'Pure Gold'.

I am gradually discovering the new role that God has
mapped out for me and it gets more exciting every day. It's

159

so beautiful to wake each morning and wonder what he has in store for me to-day.

> *If I can endure for this minute
> Whatever is happening to me,
> No matter how heavy my heart is
> Or how 'dark' the moment may be –
> If I can remain calm and quiet
> With all my world crashing about me,
> Secure in the knowledge God loves me
> When everyone else seems to doubt me –
> If I can but keep on believing
> What I know in my heart to be true,
> That 'darkness will fade with the morning'
> and that *this will pass away, too* –
> Then nothing in life can defeat me
> For as long as this knowledge remains
> I can suffer whatever is happening
> For I know God will break 'all the chains'
> That are binding me tight in *'the Darkness'*
> And trying to fill me with fear –
> For there is no *night without dawning*
> And I know that *'my morning'* is near.

*From *'Heart Gifts'* by Helen Steiner Rice. *'This too will pass away.'*